REGENTS RESTORATION DRAMA SERIES

General Editor: John Loftis

THE BEGGAR'S OPERA

JOHN GAY

The Beggar's Opera

Edited by
EDGAR V. ROBERTS

Music Edited by
EDWARD SMITH

UNIVERSITY OF NEBRASKA PRESS · LINCOLN

First Bison Book printing April, 1969
Most recent printing shown by first digit below:
3   4   5   6   7   8   9   10

MANUFACTURED IN THE UNITED STATES OF AMERICA

Regents Restoration Drama Series

The Regents Restoration Drama Series provides soundly edited texts, in modern spelling, of the more significant plays of the late seventeenth and early eighteenth centuries. The word "Restoration" is here used ambiguously and must be explained. If to the historian it refers to the period between 1660 and 1685 (or 1688), it has long been used by the student of drama in default of a more precise word to refer to plays belonging to the dramatic tradition established in the 1660's, weakening after 1700, and displaced in the 1730's. It is in this extended sense—imprecise though justified by academic custom —that the word is used in this series, which includes plays first produced between 1660 and 1737. Although these limiting dates are determined by political events, the return of Charles II (and the removal of prohibitions against operation of theaters) and the passage of Walpole's Stage Licensing Act, they enclose a period of dramatic history having a coherence of its own in the establishment, development, and disintegration of a tradition.

Some seventeen editions having appeared as this volume goes to press, the series has reached over a third of its anticipated range of between forty and fifty volumes. The volumes will continue to be published for a number of years, at the rate of three or more annually. From the beginning the editors have planned the series with attention to the projected dimensions of the completed whole, a representative collection of Restoration drama providing a record of artistic achievement and providing also a record of the deepest concerns of three generations of Englishmen. And thus it contains deservedly famous plays—*The Country Wife*, *The Man of Mode*, and *The Way of the World*—and also significant but little known plays, *The Virtuoso*, for example, and *City Politiques*, the former a satirical review of scientific investigation in the early years of the Royal Society, the latter an equally satirical review of politics at the time of the Popish Plot. If the volumes of famous plays finally achieve the larger circulation, the other volumes may conceivably have the greater utility, in making available texts otherwise difficult of access with the editorial apparatus needed to make them intelligible.

The editors have had the instructive example of the parallel and senior project, the Regents Renaissance Drama Series; they have in fact used the editorial policies developed for the earlier plays as their own, modifying them as appropriate for the later period and as the experience of successive editions suggested. The introductions to the separate Restoration plays differ considerably in their nature. Although a uniform body of relevant information is presented in each of them, no attempt has been made to impose a pattern of interpretation. Emphasis in the introductions has necessarily varied with the nature of the plays and inevitably—we think desirably—with the special interests and aptitudes of the different editors.

Each text in the series is based on a fresh collation of the seventeenth- and eighteenth-century editions that might be presumed to have authority. The textual notes, which appear above the rule at the bottom of each page, record all substantive departures from the edition used as the copy-text. Variant substantive readings among contemporary editions are listed there as well. Editions later than the eighteenth century are referred to in the textual notes only when an emendation originating in some one of them is received into the text. Variants of accidentals (spelling, punctuation, capitalization) are not recorded in the notes. Contracted forms of characters' names are silently expanded in speech prefixes and stage directions and, in the case of speech prefixes, are regularized. Additions to the stage pirections of the copy-text are enclosed in brackets.

Spelling has been modernized along consciously conservative lines, but within the limits of a modernized text the linguistic quality of the original has been carefully preserved. Contracted preterites have regularly been expanded. Punctuation has been brought into accord with modern practices. The objective has been to achieve a balance between the pointing of the old editions and a system of punctuation which, without overloading the text with exclamation marks, semicolons, and dashes, will make the often loosely flowing verse and prose of the original syntactically intelligible to the modern reader. Dashes are regularly used only to indicate interrupted speeches, or shifts of address within a single speech.

Explanatory notes, chiefly concerned with glossing obsolete words and phrases, are printed below the textual notes at the bottom of each page. References to stage directions in the notes follow the admirable system of the Revels editions, whereby stage directions are keyed, decimally, to the line of the text before or after which they occur. Thus, a note on 0.2 has reference to the second line of the stage direction at the beginning of the scene in question. A note on 115.1 has reference to the first line of the stage direction following line 115 of the text of the relevant scene. Speech prefixes, and any stage directions attached to them, are keyed to the first line of accompanying dialogue.

JOHN LOFTIS

April, 1968
Stanford University

Contents

List of Abbreviations

Bailey

Nathan Bailey. *An Universal Etymological English Dictionary*. London, 1721.

Black

Henry Campbell Black, ed. *Black's Law Dictionary*. 3rd ed. St. Paul, 1933.

Fielding

Henry Fielding. *An Enquiry into the Causes of the Late Increase of Robbers, etc. With Some Proposals for Remedying This Growing Evil*, in *The Complete Works of Henry Fielding, Esq., with an Essay . . . by William Ernest Henley*. Vol. XIII, *Legal Writings*. New York [1903, reprinted 1967].

Gee

Joshua Gee. *The Trade and Navigation of Great Britain Considered*. London, 1729.

Grose

Captain Francis Grose. *A Classical Dictionary of the Vulgar Tongue*. Ed. Eric Partridge. New York, 1963.

Holdsworth

Sir William Holdsworth. *A History of English Law*. Vol. XI. London, 1938.

Lives

Lives of the Most Remarkable Criminals, 1735. Ed. Arthur L. Hayward. London, 1927.

NC

George H. Nettleton and Arthur E. Case, eds. *British Dramatists from Dryden to Sheridan*. Boston, 1939.

Newgate Calendar

The Newgate Calendar, or Malefactors' Bloody Register. London, 1932.

O1

Octavo First Edition, 1728.

O2

"The Second Edition," Octavo, 1728.

OED

Oxford English Dictionary

om.

omitted.

Pennant

Thomas Pennant. *Some Account of London*. 2nd edn. London, 1791.

Q

"The Third Edition," Quarto, 1729.

Smith   Captain Alexander Smith. *A Complete History of the Lives and Robberies of the Most Notorious Highwaymen, Footpads, Shoplifts, and Cheats of Both Sexes.* 5th ed., 1719. Ed. Arthur L. Hayward. London, 1933.

S.D.   stage direction

S.P.   speech prefix

Thornbury   Walter Thornbury and Edward Walford. *Old and New London: A Narrative of Its History, Its People, and Its Places.* 6 vols. London, 1897.

Wild   Captain Alexander Smith. *Memoirs of the Life and Times of Jonathan Wild.* London, 1726.

Introduction

Gay sold the copyright for *The Beggar's Opera* to John Watts on February 6, 1728, eight days after the first performance on January 29, and Watts published the text in octavo (O1) on February 14.[1] The music was printed from copper plates, without words, in two separate gatherings at the end. These gatherings exist in a number of different issues and states, and a complete study would be lengthy. Briefly, however, during the press run of O1, which apparently continued for a month and a half, three separate sets of engravings of gathering G were used, along with two of gathering H. The earliest issue is represented by copies now at Harvard (*Murdock 211.5) and the Huntington Library ([Huth-Chew] 144496). There are two transitional issues, as in copies at Harvard (*15459.628.10) and the Folger Shakespeare Library (PR/3473/B3/1728/Cage). Copies of the last issue, which seems to be the most common, are at Harvard (*15459.628.20), Huntington (K–D 141), and the University of Texas Library (WK./G252/728 ba). Few of the copies are identical, for minor changes were made in the plates during the run of the presses. At the time the last engravings of the music were in the press, an additional song (Air LVI, "Ourselves, like the great," to the music of "A Cobbler There Was") was included in the text itself, on page 53, with music printed by a wood-block method. To accommodate this alteration, the standing type of O1 was re-arranged.

[1] Walter E. Knotts, "Press Numbers as a Bibliographical Tool: A Study of Gay's *The Beggar's Opera*, 1728," *Harvard Library Bulletin*, III (1949), 209, 204. There has been uncertainty about the sequence of the first-edition issues. The interested reader can study the various claims in Thomas J. Wise, *The Ashley Library, a Catalogue of Printed Books, Manuscripts and Autograph Letters*, II (1923), 140 f.; in Knotts's article; and in William B. Todd's review of Knotts's article in *Philological Quarterly*, XXIX (1950), 238–240. Brief bibliographical accounts of the various editions of *The Beggar's Opera* may be found in George H. Nettleton and Arthur E. Case, eds., *British Dramatists from Dryden to Sheridan* (Boston, 1939); in G. C. Faber, ed., *The Poetical Works of John Gay* (London, 1926); and in *The Rothschild Library: A Catalogue of the Collection of Eighteenth-Century Printed Books and Manuscripts Formed by Lord Rothschild* (Cambridge, 1954).

The play-reading public, however, apparently demanded music and lyrics together, and as a result a second octavo edition was published on April 9. This is O2, the second authorized edition, which up to Act III, scene viii was printed largely with standing type from O1. The main feature of O2 was the inclusion of the music "prefix'd to each song." In this format, each complete melody was printed by the same wood-block method as was the new song in O1, and the appropriate song was then printed as a lyric poem immediately below. This format became standard for most of the ballad operas published in subsequent years by John Watts. The text of O2 underwent several substantive changes, namely, (1) the alteration of a sentence in I.vi, (2) the addition of *have* in the first line of Air VII, (3) the continuous numbering of the airs throughout the play, (4) the addition of a sentence in II.iv, and (5) the change (during the press run) of *weary* to *wary* in Air XL.

A still different method of printing the music characterized the sumptuous third, quarto, edition of 1729, which reproduced the text of O2. This is Q, the last edition authorized in Gay's lifetime. In Q, the music was printed from copper plates and included separately at the end of the play, with the words (which were also included in the text itself) printed directly below the proper musical notes. Also included were single-note bass accompaniments by Dr. John Christopher Pepusch, who directed the orchestra during the first season of *The Beggar's Opera*. The musical format of Q has proved fortunate, because it provides modern readers with the exact way in which most of the songs were fitted to the music, and the indication of how refrains and repeats were sung. Though the relationship of Pepusch's basses to his orchestrations for the first performances of *The Beggar's Opera* cannot now be determined, these basses were played by many amateur musicians in the eighteenth century. The full keyboard accompaniments included in Appendix A are realizations of these basses.[2]

The copy-text of the present edition is a copy of O1 in the Harvard University Library (*Murdock 211.5). The authority of Lockit's song in III.xi (Air LVI) is also in Harvard (*15459.628.20). Depar-

---

[2] Dr. Burney called these basses "so excellent, that no sound contrapuntist will ever attempt to alter them," though his judgment has not met with universal acceptance (Charles Burney, *A General History of Music From the Earliest Ages to the Present Period* [*1789*], critical and historical notes by Frank Mercer [New York, 1935, reprinted 1957], II, 986).

tures from the copy-text include the changes that appeared in O2 and
Q. To this text, necessary stage directions have been added in square
brackets. The text has been collated with six other copies of O1
from the Harvard Library, three from the Yale University Library,
one from the Folger Shakespeare Library, three from the Henry E.
Huntington Library, one from the British Museum, and four from
the University of Texas Library. In addition, the text has been
collated with the two most important modern editions of *The Beggar's
Opera*: those in the Nettleton-Case anthology (NC) and in G. C.
Faber, ed., *The Poetical Works of John Gay* (Oxford, 1926). Collation
has brought to light no substantive variants, though O1 itself exists in a
number of separate states characterized by unimportant variants in
accidentals. As might be expected, the play was pirated, and there
were Dublin editions, but because these editions were unauthorized,
they have not been consulted in the establishment of the present text.

By the time *The Beggar's Opera* was written and produced, con-
ditions in the London theater were ripe for satire. The audiences had
an established taste for farcical afterpieces (short plays following the
main attraction) and also for a good deal of preludial music and
entr'acte song and dance. So pressing was their demand for variety
that occasionally the theater managers shortened the regular five-act
plays in order to provide it. Advertisements in the London papers
attempted to attract crowds by naming the main *entr'acte* performers:
Leveridge or Mrs. Chambers, for example, to sing; Dupre or Mrs.
Brett to dance. Pantomine, that combination of music and dance, was
popular with the average theater-goer; Italian operas, principally
those by George Frederick Handel, had gained prestige among the
upper classes. *The Beggar's Opera* is a satire upon all these forms of
entertainment; moreover, it is at the same time an original new art
form—the "ballad opera."[3]

This happy fusion of music and drama created a demand for more
plays in the form. As Gay first fashioned it, and as it was followed
by other authors writing in imitation of him, the ballad opera was an
irregular play (that is, a three-act mainpiece or an afterpiece of one
of two acts) which was frequently satiric but also sometimes pastoral
or farcical. Its dialogue was spoken, not sung in recitative as in the
Italian operas, and its principal characteristic was the integral use

[3] See Edmond McAdoo Gagey, *Ballad Opera* (New York, 1937), for a
history and study of the form.

of many songs which were fitted to already popular ballad tunes (though occasionally some of the music was specially composed). Many of the tunes were of genuine folk origin, but a greater number were in fact drawing-room and street ballads, and the great bulk of these were of recent composition. Naturally, the introduction of music provided opportunities for dance and spectacle.

The creation of the ballad-opera form was a considerable achievement in itself. With time and modification it has been extended to such diverse works as the *Singspiele* of Mozart, the Savoy operas, and the collaborations of Rogers and Hammerstein.[4] The historical consequences of Gay's play have been even more extensive. Its melodies, a collection of spirited and sometimes hauntingly beautiful songs drawn mainly from English music, contributed as much to the developing interest in popular poetry and music as did the later *Reliques* of Bishop Percy and the earlier critiques of "Chevy Chase" by Addison. Today, *The Beggar's Opera* is for most students the principal locus of seventeenth- and eighteenth-century popular music.

As the play came from Gay's pen in 1727, however, before time conferred such favor upon it, it was a doubtful quantity. Its novelty caused Gay's friends who read it in advance of production to question what the public response would be. Their consensus was the safe one, most memorably and vacuously expressed by Gay's friend and patron, the Duke of Queensberry: "This is a very odd thing, Gay; I am satisfied that it is either a very good thing, or a very bad thing."[5] Gay himself doubted that the public would like the work, and he prepared himself for possible failure by disclaiming concern about its reception.[6] Doubts were not limited to his circle, for he had difficulty in getting the play accepted at either of the major theaters. Colley

---

[4] See Jeffrey Mark, "Ballad Opera and its Significance in the History of English Stage-Music," *London Mercury*, VIII (1923), 256–278; and my "Eighteenth-Century Ballad Opera: The Contribution of Henry Fielding," *Drama Survey*, I (1961), 77–79.

[5] This remark, reported by the Duke to Boswell, is recorded in *The Life of Johnson* under the date April 18, 1775 (*Boswell's Life of Johnson*, ed. George Birkbeck Hill and revised by L. F. Powell [Oxford, 1934], II, 368; cited in William Eben Schultz, *Gay's Beggar's Opera: Its Content, History, and Influence* [New Haven, 1923], p. 125).

[6] In a letter to Swift in January, 1728, Pope wrote, "At worst it [*The Beggar's Opera*] is in its own nature a thing which he [Gay] can *lose* no reputation by, as he lays none upon it" (*The Correspondence of Alexander Pope*, ed. George Sherburn [Oxford, 1956], II, 469).

Cibber, who judged plays submitted to the Theatre Royal in Drury Lane, rejected it. After this disappointment, Gay offered the play to John Rich, the English Harlequin, at Lincoln's Inn Fields. Though Rich was reluctant, he decided to risk production.[7]

Once the play had been accepted, there were doubts about how it should be produced. During the early rehearsals, the actors sang unaccompanied, apparently at Gay's insistence. Because the theater's orchestra was available, however, and perhaps because the actors needed instrumental support, Gay was persuaded to allow orchestral accompaniments.[8] These were composed, along with an overture, by the music director at Lincoln's Inn Fields, Dr. Pepusch.[9] Though

[7] Gay claimed, in a letter to Swift of February 17, 1728, that he had "push'd through this precarious Affair without servility or flattery . . ." (*The Letters of John Gay*, ed. C. F. Burgess [Oxford, 1966], p. 70). In the same letter, he stated that "The Duchess of Queensberry hath signaliz'd her friendship to me upon this occasion in . . . a conspicuous manner . . . ." The second statement has apparently been taken to mean that the Duchess promised to repay any losses Rich might have incurred in producing *The Beggar's Opera*. Gay's biographer, William Henry Irving, relates this interpretation as fact, citing the letter mentioned above as his only supporting evidence (*John Gay, Favorite of the Wits* [Durham, 1940, reprinted 1962], pp. 240 f.). Schultz presents the same interpretation with no apparent authority (pp. 1 f.). The interpretation is discussed, again without documentation, in Phoebe Fenwick Gaye, *John Gay: His Place in the Eighteenth Century* (London, 1938), pp. 321 f., and is offered as truth in the introduction to C. F. Burgess, ed., *The Beggar's Opera and Companion Pieces* (New York, 1966), p. viii, and elsewhere. Despite these many accounts, it is difficult to see how Gay's words can be interpreted in such a manner without further evidence.

[8] This statement is based upon an anecdote in William Cooke, *Memoirs of Charles Macklin Comedian, with the Dramatic Characters, Manners, &c. of the Age in Which He Lived* (London, 1804), which has it that the decision to include orchestral accompaniments was not made until the final rehearsal, and then only at the insistence of the Duchess of Queensberry (p. 60). Cooke's *Memoirs* did not appear until seventy-six years after *The Beggar's Opera*, however, and the factual basis for his story may be no more than that the orchestra was not brought in to the rehearsals until shortly before the first performance, a common practice. It is also possible that the orchestra was originally intended to accompany only some of the songs, and that the decision to provide accompaniments for all of them was made after rehearsals began. For further discussion of the anecdote, see Schultz, pp. 126 f. On the orchestra at Lincoln's Inn Fields, see Emmett L. Avery, ed., *The London Stage, 1660–1800, Part Two: 1700–1729* (Carbondale, Ill., 1960), I, cxxxvii.

[9] On Pepusch's career, see Charles W. Hughes, "John Christopher Pepusch," *Musical Quarterly*, XXXI (1945), 54–70.

later productions have emphasized a *parlando* delivery by some of the actors (and certainly the original Peachum, John Hippisley, must have been a better actor than singer), the two main actors were apparently chosen because of their ability to sing. James Quin rejected the role of Macheath after rehearsing it briefly, and Rich then gave the part to Thomas Walker, a younger actor with a better singing voice.[10] The role of Polly was taken by an unknown young actress, Lavinia Fenton, whose talent and beauty quickly made her the darling of the Town—and of a noble lord.[11]

The preparations and uncertainty presumably gave notice that much was to be expected of the play. Gay's friends went to the theater for the first night's performance, together with "a prodigious Concourse of Nobility and Gentry," and many others.[12] Even the first Minister, Walpole, was in the house. The response of the almost thirteen hundred persons present on the first night has been described by a number of witnesses. The gist of their accounts is that the early part of the play was received coolly, but beginning either at Polly's Air XII ("Now Ponder Well") or at the gang's chorus in Act II (Air XX, "Let Us Take the Road"), the audience applauded, and then greeted the remainder of the play with enthusiastic ovations.[13] As interesting as the accounts are, they are probably more anecdotal than historical. The audience was not hostile, and did not need great convincing. If indeed those present took some time to be won over by *The Beggar's Opera*, their delay was probably caused by a need to

10 Genest, however, asserts that Walker "knew no more of singing than to sing in tune" (*Some Account of the English Stage* [Bath, 1832], III, 221).

11 Charles E. Pearce, *"Polly Peachum," Being the Story of Lavinia Fenton (Duchess of Bolton) and "The Beggar's Opera"* (London, 1913), p. 223.

12 *The Daily Journal*, Feb. 1, 1728, quoted in Irving, p. 256, and in Gagey, p. 35. Avery, II, 956–981, gives the receipts and attendance figures for the first night and for each night's performance until the end of the season on June 19.

13 Quin told Richard Cambridge, who told Boswell, that the audience did not respond until Polly's Air (*Life of Johnson*, II, 368); Cooke's *Memoirs of Macklin* is the source of the story that the gang's chorus occasioned the first ovation (p. 57). Both Pope (in Joseph Spence, *Observations, Anecdotes, and Characters of Books and Men*, ed. James M. Osborn [Oxford, 1966], I, 107 f.) and Benjamin Victor (*The History of the Theatres of London and Dublin, From the Year 1730 to the Present Time* [London, 1761], p. 154) agree that the audience's approval was delayed. Because the play was new, however, one might reasonably have expected such a delay. Schultz (pp. 3–5) cites all the anecdotes about the first night's performance.

adjust to the musical innovation of the ballad-opera form, not by any doubt about the play's excellence. No matter how long the audience waited to show its entire approval, however, the first night's reception assured success for Gay and the producer, Rich, during the following months. With time out for the usual spring benefits, the play was performed at Lincoln's Inn Fields a total of sixty-two times before the season closed on June 19, by far the most extensive first run of any play to that date on the English stage. Gay himself earned close to £800 from his benefits and from the sale of his copyright, a very large sum.

This sum was only the material form of Gay's success. Prior to the first performance he had been known as the author of moderately successful plays and the successful poems *Trivia*, *The Shepherd's Week*, and the first series of *The Fables*. He was not without important friends, among others Swift, Pope, and Arbuthnot—the "Tory Satirists"; he was patronized by the Duke and Duchess of Queensberry, and was befriended by Mrs. Howard, the King's reputed mistress, and also by many other "persons of quality." He had the minor post of Commissioner of the English state lottery, and had been recently offered a minor position in the royal household, which he had refused. By the end of the first run of *The Beggar's Opera*, however, his reputation as one of the country's first authors was assured. He spent his remaining four years at the peak of fame, and when he died in 1732 he was acknowledged as a celebrity. He was buried with ceremony in the Poets' Corner of Westminster Abbey.

The fame awarded *The Beggar's Opera* by Gay's contemporaries was justified by its vitality and memorable originality; the play remains as impressive today as when Gay wrote it. Even its satire on politics and society still has power and relevance. The play was one of the earliest works in which an unusual social setting was integrated with plot—as subsequently in the novels of Dickens and Hardy. Gay took his subject matter from the criminal life of the early eighteenth century, perhaps following a hint by Swift, who eleven years before *The Beggar's Opera* had suggested in a letter to Pope that Gay might write a "Newgate pastoral, among the whores and thieves there."[14]

14 *The Correspondence of Jonathan Swift*, ed. Harold Williams (Oxford, 1963), II, 215. This letter, of August 30, 1716, is frequently cited. For a full discussion of the origins of *The Beggar's Opera*, see Irving, pp. 228–235, and C. F. Burgess, "The Genesis of *The Beggar's Opera*," *Cithara*, II (1962), 6–12.

Yet if Gay's characters are low, they are preeminently dramatis personae in a well-wrought play, and do not possess merely the negative qualities of their class. Following mock-epic convention, Gay endowed them with the speech of shopkeepers and businessmen, and even, in the case of Macheath, with the speech of protagonists of heroic plays. The characters possess an entertaining effrontery that gives constant surprise. The dramatization is realistic, however, to the extent that the action portrays the antagonism and injustice existing within the criminal class.

The conflict among the thieves, as a symbol of the world at large, is a major basis of Gay's political satire: as Peachum, with the immunity of power, uses the gang for his own ends, so the government of Gay's time, above all the first Minister, Walpole, exploited the people. Peachum represents Walpole in his capacity as businessman and administrator. He is a parasite, like many characters in earlier comedy, as is shown in his first speech:

> A lawyer is an honest employment; so is mine. Like me too he acts in a double capacity, both against rogues and for 'em; for 'tis but fitting that we should protect and encourage cheats, since we live by them.[15]

The parasite is a type who preys upon the other characters, frequently inveighing against the evils of which he himself is guilty, and always attempting to preserve respectability.[16] In Gay's eyes, Walpole had provided justification for the satiric portrayal by his machinations to acquire and retain power, his profiteering from South-Sea stock, his use of patronage and bribery, and his elimination of potential political rivals.

Gay satirizes Walpole by other means; his method, in fact, has been well described as "rotating" because he strikes first through one character, and then through another.[17] He ridicules Walpole not

---

[15] I.i.9–12.

[16] For a discussion of the parasite in satire, see Rose A. Zimbardo, *Wycherley's Drama: A Link in the Development of English Satire* (*Yale Studies in English*, Vol. 156 [New Haven, 1965]), pp. 72–96.

[17] Schultz, p. 197. John Loftis, in *The Politics of Drama in Augustan England* (Oxford, 1963), succinctly states that the play "scores its hits by way of a succession of political parallels, each established briefly and then obscured as different character relationships emerge" (p. 94). See also C. F. Burgess, "Political Satire: John Gay's *The Beggar's Opera*," *Midwest Quarterly*, VI (1965), 270–274.

only through Peachum, but also through names like *Bluff Bob*, *Bob Booty*, and *Robin of Bagshot* (I.iii), and more importantly through Macheath. That Macheath is a vehicle of political satire may seem at first surprising: he is an engaging character and he is an antagonist of Peachum, who also represents Walpole. Yet at the time of *The Beggar's Opera*, it was assumed that Macheath, the aristocratic "Captain" of the gang, represented the "Prime Minister" of the courtiers. There were other good reasons for the identification. Though Macheath is a dashing figure never seen in the vicious act of committing a robbery, he is always a highwayman. Walpole's alleged peculations were always performed silently behind the mask of his official position. Both were, in plain words, nothing more than thieves. Macheath's involvement with Polly and Lucy suggested the first Minister's extramarital affair with Molly Skerrit (whom he eventually married). Macheath's reprieve from hanging suggested the allegation that Walpole's political life, apparently ended in 1727 when George II succeeded, was saved by an ingenious manipulation of the Civil-List money.[18] It goes virtually without saying, however, that neither Macheath nor Peachum has merely allegorical significance in the play.

Upon close examination, Gay's satire yields other riches than the attack upon Walpole. The values upon which the satire is based were those that led Englishmen toward social reform in the decades following the play, and which were incorporated in democratic theories later in the century. Gay's obvious sympathy for Macheath and the gang indicates a basic assumption—the standard by which the satire may be measured—that there is much to admire in men, but that genuine goodness can be brought out only through a sensitive and responsible social system. In the eighteenth-century world, it was considered a paternal duty for the upper class to nurture the lower classes. Gay felt that this obligation had not been met, and his play offers a clever protest. *The Beggar's Opera* argues satirically that arbitrary and self-seeking enforcement of laws baffles human potential by directing men away from the cultivation of goodness into the channel of survival by any means, including crime. While society at large cries out for help, men of power, exemplified satirically by Peachum and the jailer, Lockit, fill their pockets and look the other

[18] *Lord Hervey's Memoirs*, ed. Romney Sedgwick, rev. edn. (New York, 1963), pp. 6–9. Cf. also J. H. Plumb, *Sir Robert Walpole, the King's Minister* (Boston, 1961), pp. 168 f.

way. Such corruption cannot damage human energy—witness Macheath and the gang—but it does produce poverty and crime.

Yet Gay's ideas are clearly not democratic or socialistic, as some writers have suggested,[19] but are broadly Christian and humanitarian. Gay was no egalitarian, no revolutionary; he was a man of his time. He did not will the demise of his aristocratic friends as a class; rather, he admired their virtues. Though his own political disappointments may have sharpened his resentment of those in power, it by no means follows that he aimed *The Beggar's Opera* at the destruction of the social and political system he knew. He aimed rather at the abuses within the system, and his satirical theme is the conservative one that correction should come through reform rather than revolt.

To Gay, as to Swift and Pope, social reform began within the individual, who could be reached and improved by satire. It was important, psychologically and politically, that each individual identify his own interests with those of society at large. Swift's ideal political projectors in Part Three of *Gulliver's Travels* teach princes "to know their true Interest, by placing it on the same Foundation with that of their People."[20] If each man merged "Self-love" with "Social," in Pope's words, and reinforced this "proper operation"[21] with Christian morality, his life would then be characterized by magnanimity. This ideal inspired Pope's portrait of the benevolent Man of Ross in the *Epistle to Bathurst*, published five years after *The Beggar's Opera*. The Man of Ross, one might recall, carried out conservation projects, public works, and social welfare; he practiced medicine and law, without charge, as a public service.[22] Ideally,

[19] Sven M. Armens, *John Gay, Social Critic* (New York, 1954), p. 56 (but see p. 57); Schultz, pp. 198 f.; and Bertrand H. Bronson, "The Beggar's Opera," in *Studies in the Comic* (*University of California Publications in English*, Vol. VIII, No. 2, 1941), pp. 227 f. (reprinted in John Loftis, ed., *Restoration Drama: Modern Essays in Criticism* [New York, 1966], pp. 298–327). Professor Bronson's article provides the best evaluation of *The Beggar's Opera*.

[20] *Gulliver's Travels, 1726,* intro. by Harold Williams (*The Prose Works of Jonathan Swift*, ed. Herbert Davis, Vol. XI [Oxford: Basil Blackwell, 1941]), p. 171.

[21] *An Essay on Man*, III, 318, and II, 57, in *An Essay on Man*, ed. Maynard Mack (*The Twickenham Edition of the Poems of Alexander Pope*, gen. ed. John Butt, Vol. III, Part i [London, 1950]), pp. 126, 62.

[22] Lines 249–274, in *Epistles to Several Persons* (*Moral Essays*), ed. F. W. Bateson (*The Twickenham Edition of the Poems of Alexander Pope*, gen. ed. John Butt, Vol. III, Part ii [London, 1951]), pp. 110–112.

from such individual goodness a healthy society would spring. The laws, which were "made for ev'ry degree,"[23] would be impartially enforced, and justice would prevail.

Such, however, was far from the case. The lawyers and statesmen of Gay's world outlawed and hanged men like Macheath; the absentee English landlords of Swift's world exploited their Irish tenants; the aristocratic classes of Pope's world engaged in conspicuous and vulgar consumption. Men everywhere failed to see that unbridled self-interest was incompatible with reason and morality, or, if they did see, they failed to act upon their knowledge. In the opinion of Gay, Swift, and Pope, society was stagnant, the poor becoming more wretched and the rich more irresponsible.

One manifestation of spiritual waste, in the satirist's view, was the pursuit of ostentatious diversions. The upper classes, derelict in their role, had even deserted native English forms of dramatic art, preferring the unstructured and sentimental plots of Italian operas (which often had overtures in the French style) to the tightly wrought plays of the Elizabethan Jonson and of the more recent Wycherley and Congreve. Hence Gay satirizes Italian opera: *The Beggar's Opera*, written in English, uses common ballads, occasional *bravura* passages, songs burlesquing the "simile" songs of opera, and scenes reminiscent of those in specific operas.[24] It includes no recitative, and Pepusch's overture is composed in the French style. These elements, to name only the most significant, are the vehicles of Gay's satire. Ever since Addison's brilliant *Spectator* paper on Nicolini and the lion,[25] repeated attacks had been made on Italian opera; nevertheless, the opera held its audiences. In 1728, however, the Royal Academy of Music, which since 1720 had produced operas at the King's Theatre in the Haymarket, was undergoing a financial crisis and other internal difficulties. Gay's ridicule probably hurt attendance, and the Academy abandoned opera, and Handel, during the next season. For this reason, and also because Gay had proved that an English musical play could be popular, *The Beggar's Opera* may have

[23] Air LXVII of *The Beggar's Opera* (III.xiii.22).

[24] Bronson, pp. 204–217. See also Arthur V. Berger, "*The Beggar's Opera*, the Burlesque, and Italian Opera," *Music and Letters*, XVII (1936), 93–105.

[25] *Spectator*, No. 13, in Donald F. Bond, ed., *The Spectator* (Oxford, 1965), I, 55–59. See also No. 18 (I, 78–82) and Steele's remarks on opera in No. 14 (I, 63–65).

influenced Handel's turning from Italian opera in the 1730's to dramatic oratorios for English libretti.

Just as *The Beggar's Opera* is in one of its aspects a burlesque of Italian opera, it is in another a burlesque of the sensational criminal literature that had developed in England during the early years of the century. It is a satire upon the lurid and the cheap, such as the collection of semi-biographical criminal tales by Captain Alexander Smith, *A Complete History of the Lives and Robberies of the Most Notorious Highwaymen, Footpads, Shoplifts, and Cheats of Both Sexes* (1714), which was expanded for its fifth edition in 1719. This edition contained accounts of 137 criminals, together with a glossary and grammar of low-life language. As a conventional justification for each biography, the author moralized about the brutality and folly of the criminal life. The public appetite which supported the five editions of this collection was profitably fed by John Applebee, a publisher who issued many pamphlet lives of criminals in the following years. Interest in the sensational aspects of criminal life reached a peak in the 1720's with the hanging of Jonathan Wild, whose organizational genius in the dual capacity of receiver of stolen goods and thief-catcher was never matched, and Jack Sheppard, whose spectacular escapes from Newgate were unprecedented. In part because of Defoe's biographical accounts of them,[26] these men captured the public imagination as no rogues had previously done. They caught Gay's imagination, too; it is apparent that Wild was the model for Peachum, and Sheppard for Macheath. An unreliable anecdote has it that Gay met Wild one night in an inn, and thus learned about criminal habits from the most authoritative source available.[27] In any event, Gay did acquire much knowledge of criminal life, and in 1725 he published "Newgate's Garland," a song inspired by the attempted murder of Wild by a cutthroat named Blueskin, which suggested ironically that the activities of gentlemen and of rogues were not without their similarities.[28]

[26] *The True and Genuine Account of the Life and Actions of the Late Jonathan Wild* (London, 1725), and *A Narrative of All the Robberies, Escapes, etc. of John Sheppard* (London, 1724).

[27] James R. Sutherland, "The Beggar's Opera," *Times Literary Supplement*, April 25, 1935, p. 272. Irving (pp. 235 f.) discusses Newgate drama prior to *The Beggar's Opera*.

[28] G. C. Faber, ed., *Works*, pp. 186–188. Harold Williams (*The Poems of Jonathan Swift* [Oxford, 1937]) argues that this poem is by Swift (III, 1111–1113). Faber grants that stanzas six and seven were Swift's, but

Gay's satiric stance in *The Beggar's Opera*, particularly his exposure of criminal hypocrisy, establishes the play as a parody of the criminal "biographies." These tales began with an account of each criminal's initiation into crime, and followed his career to his execution. *The Beggar's Opera* differs in structure, but it includes all the details of the typical criminal life, and it satirizes the romantic belief in honor among thieves. Except for Polly and Lucy, the dramatis personae are criminals: highwaymen, pickpockets, housebreakers, prostitutes, a receiver of stolen goods, a corrupt jailer, and a bawd. They drink, argue, fight, and wench. The dramatic action, set amid low scenes, develops from Peachum's conspiracy with Mrs. Peachum to bring Macheath to the gallows. The characters emphasize the proximity of violent death, often referring to the cart which carried condemned prisoners to Tyburn and then served as the platform to be driven away from under them after they had been strung up. Gay, however, always preserves a comic tone. Although he includes vicious deeds as an element in his parody, he does not expose criminal viciousness. Instead he emphasizes the hypocrisy of his characters, for his satire is aimed not at the vices of the criminal but at the modes of the Court. "L'hypocrisie," wrote La Rochefoucauld, "est un hommage que le vice rend à la vertu."[29]

The one action lacking in *The Beggar's Opera* to complete the dramatized pattern of the criminal tale—an omission important in establishing that the play is a parody rather than a romantic rendering of low life—is the death by hanging of one of the principal characters. Yet, as is suggested by the reference to the fate of Matt of the Mint's brother Tom (II.i), the threat of hanging is always present, and Macheath escapes only because of the comic reprieve. If Gay's next ballad opera, *Polly*, is accepted as Gay intended it—as a sequel to *The Beggar's Opera*—then the criminal tale is completed. In *Polly*, published in 1729 after its production was prohibited by Walpole's friend the Lord Chamberlain, the deaths of Peachum and Macheath are reported.

The inclusion of these deaths in *Polly* suggests that what was to become a long tradition of deploring *The Beggar's Opera* on moral

---

attributes the rest of the poem to Gay (*Works*, pp. xxvi f.). Irving believes that the poem is by Gay (pp. 203–207).

[29] *Réflexion* No. 218, in La Rochefoucauld, *Oeuvres Complètes*, ed. L. Martin-Chauffier (Bibliothèque de la Pléiade, Vol. XXIV [Tours, 1950]), p. 276.

grounds had begun, and that Gay had been troubled by the adverse criticism.[30] Shortly after the Town had taken *The Beggar's Opera* to heart, the Reverend Thomas Herring preached an influential sermon against it as a "thing of every evil tendency."[31] Others apparently claimed that Gay had "given up" his "moral for a joke."[32] His jocular tone was found to be objectionable—his depiction of Macheath the highwayman, for example, as an amusing if somewhat irresponsible young man.

Against this censure, Swift vigorously and ironically defended his friend:

> In this happy Performance of Mr. GAY's, all the Characters are just, and none of them carried beyond Nature, or hardly beyond Practice. It discovers the whole System of that Common-Wealth, or that *Imperium in Imperio* of Iniquity, established among us, by which neither our Lives nor our Properties are secure, either in the High-ways, or in publick Assemblies, or even in our own Houses. It shews the miserable Lives and the constant Fate of those abandoned Wretches: For how little they sell their Lives and Souls; betrayed by their *Whores*, their *Comrades*, and the *Receivers* and *Purchasers* of those Thefts and Robberies. This *Comedy* contains likewise a *Satyr*, which, without enquiring whether it affects the present Age, may possibly be useful in Times to come. I mean, where the Author takes the Occasion of comparing those *common Robbers of the Publick*, and their several Stratagems of betraying, undermining and hanging each other, to the several Arts of *Politicians* in Times of Corruption.[33]

Swift's defense, like Gay's own in the preliminaries to *Polly*, was to grant the critical premise that literature should be moral, but to insist that satire was a legitimate way of supporting morality. Gay

[30] In March, 1729, Gay wrote to Swift: "For writing in the cause of Virtue and against the fashionable vices, I am look'd upon at present as the most obnoxious person almost in England, Mr Pulteney tells me I have got the start of him. Mr Pope tells me that I am dead and that this obnoxiousness is the reward for my inoffensiveness in my former life" (*The Letters of John Gay*, p. 80).

[31] *Mist's Weekly Journal*, March 30, 1728. Quoted in Schultz, p. 227.

[32] Introduction to *Polly*, in *Works*, p. 537. See also Irving, p. 270.

[33] *The Intelligencer*, No. 3, May 25, 1728, in *Irish Tracts, 1728–1733* (*The Prose Works of Jonathan Swift*, ed. Herbert Davis, Vol. XII [Oxford: Basil Blackwell, 1955]), p. 36.

wrote that his aim in *Polly* was "to lash in general the reigning and fashionable vices, and to recommend and set virtue in as amiable a light as . . . [he] could." The remark is equally applicable to the satire of *The Beggar's Opera*.

The play's defenders have sometimes used misleading arguments in support of it. Dr. Johnson conceded in conversation with Boswell that *The Beggar's Opera* could create a harmful effect by "making the character of a rogue familiar, and in some degree pleasing," but he doubted that it had ever done so. Johnson delivered a more decisive opinion in his *Lives of the English Poets*: "The play, like many others, was plainly written only to divert, without any moral purpose, and is therefore not likely to do good; nor can it be conceived, without more speculation than life requires or admits, to be productive of much evil." [34] This argument, which succeeds only by emasculating Gay's satire, has provided a major defense ever since Johnson wrote it. To many critics, it has seemed the only defense. William Eben Schultz, for example, whose *Gay's Beggar's Opera* is the most comprehensive source of information about the play, states that "Gay intended no moral in *The Beggar's Opera*, no serious message for his time." [35] In order to justify chapters like "Political Satire" and "Social Satire," however, Schultz concedes that the play contains "some sound satirical advice thrown in for good measure." [36]

One may reasonably suppose that Gay would have been distressed by defenses of his work which minimize his satire. *The Beggar's Opera* is moral, but not platitudinous; its theme is presented wittily and ironically, and it forces a restatement of what constitutes morality. Gay's satire is the avenue to his moral position, and it is here that the vigor of *The Beggar's Opera* (and the weakness of *Polly*) lies.

In any consideration of *The Beggar's Opera*, then, one must remember that it is above all a satire, though it is also a ballad opera, a "Newgate Pastoral," and a parody of both Italian opera and criminal literature. In addition to the topical attack upon the government, Gay assaults virtually every social and moral assumption of the upper classes from which the government came. The first

---

34 *Boswell's Life of Johnson*, under Tuesday, April 18, 1775 (II, 367), and *Lives of the English Poets by Samuel Johnson, LL.D.*, ed. George Birkbeck Hill (Oxford, 1905), II, 278.

35 Schultz, p. 268.

36 *Ibid.* Irving emphatically declares that "The play has no morals!" (p. 251).

moment in Peachum's shop creates the comic inversion; here is the fence, declaring that his is a business like any other, one of the "employments of life." In his own peculiar world he is at the top of the Great Chain, as it were, of Criminal Being. Gay implies that all of society, and not merely those inhabiting the colorful and tuneful underworld, should be weighed in the same scale.

Granted this premise, the play offers a series of new illuminations: Who, having seen that Peachum is as important in Gay's under-world as the professional men in polite society, can ever again take these men so seriously? Who, having looked at marriage through the eyes of Mr. and Mrs. Peachum (who are as conventional within their code as the family of any merchant), can ever again see it in a totally solemn fashion? Who, having observed the code by which the criminals operate successfully, can deny that this code may be followed just as successfully in the way of life that men consider honest?

Despite the moral censure sometimes provoked by Gay's jocular tone, *The Beggar's Opera* has always been acclaimed in the theater. Throughout the eighteenth century there were annual revivals, and many of the leading actors and actresses prided themselves on their interpretations of the roles of Macheath and Polly. The popularity of the play continued in the next century until about 1885. Owing largely to the enthusiasm following the successful revival in 1920 at the Lyric Theatre in Hammersmith, *The Beggar's Opera* has entered the modern repertory. Performances by amateur and professional troupes have been legion, and in 1953 the play was made into a motion picture with Sir Laurence Olivier as Macheath. Bertholt Brecht followed Gay's plot and re-created many of Gay's characters in his *Die Dreigroschenoper* (*The Threepenny Opera*, 1928), with new music in the jazz idiom by Kurt Weill (who retained one of Gay's melodies, Air I). Both the composer Benjamin Britten and the musicologist Edward J. Dent orchestrated the tunes of *The Beggar's Opera*. However, the best-known orchestration, though abridged, is that made by Sir Frederic Austin for the Hammersmith production. A shortened version of the play with the Austin music has been recorded a number of times in the last thirty years. A complete performance of the music with the orchestration of Max Goberman has also been recorded, although the production of the play itself in this recording is discontinuous. *The Beggar's Opera* has thus reached a wide modern audience, wider perhaps that that of any other eighteenth-century play. What Johnson said of Shakespeare's works may not inappropriately be applied to Gay's triumphant ballad opera:

> What mankind have long possessed they have often examined and compared; and if they persist to value the possession, it is because frequent comparisons have confirmed opinion in its favour.[37]

EDGAR V. ROBERTS

Herbert H. Lehman College
of The City University of New York

A NOTE ON THE ORIGINS OF THE TUNES

The title preceding each air is the original name of the tune (except for Airs XXXII ["Walsingham"] and XXXVII, for which Gay did not provide titles). Histories of these tunes are numerous. By far the best work is Claude M. Simpson, *The British Broadside Ballad and Its Music* (New Brunswick, 1966). Professor Simpson discusses the forty-one tunes used by Gay that are usually called "broadside" or "black-letter" ballads. These are Airs I (indexed as "Kind Husband and Imperious Wife"), II, III (as "Stingo"), V, VI, VII, VIII, X, XI, XII (as "Children in the Wood"), XIV, XVI, XVII (as "The Broom, the Bonny Broom"), XXIII (as "The Friar and the Nun"), XXIV (as "The King's Delight"), XXV (as "All in the Land of Cyder"), XXVI, XXVII, XXVIII, XXIX (as "The Hemp Dresser"), XXI, XXXII (as "Walsingham"), XXXIII (as "Ladies of London"), XXXV (as "The Rant"), XLI, XLIII, XLIV, XLV (as "Ah Cruel Bloody Fate"), XLIX (as "A Health to Betty"), LI, LIII, LIV (as "Come Hither, My Own Sweet Duck"), LV, LVI (as "Derry Down"), LVII, LXI, LXII, LXIII (as "Farinel's Ground"), LXV (as "I Live Not Where I Love"), LXVI, and LXVII. However, since Professor Simpson is concerned only with the broadside tunes, he does not discuss twenty-eight of the tunes appearing in *The Beggar's Opera*. His work may therefore be supplemented by A. E. H. Swaen

[37] "Preface to Shakespeare" (1765), in *Johnson on Shakespeare*, ed. Sir Walter Raleigh (London, 1925), pp. 9 f.

INTRODUCTION

("The Airs and Tunes of John Gay's Beggar's Opera," *Anglia*, XLIII [1919], 152–190), Frank Kidson (*The Beggar's Opera: Its Predecessors and Successors* [Cambridge, 1922]), and William E. Schultz (*Gay's Beggar's Opera: Its Content, History, and Influence* [New Haven, 1923]), who present histories of all the tunes, though their work is less reliable than is Professor Simpson's. Most of the tunes are discussed in two books by the nineteenth-century ballad scholar, William Chappell (*A Collection of National English Airs* [London, 1838–1840], and *Popular Music of the Olden Time* [London, 1855–1859]). There is also a discussion of the tunes by Max Goberman in *The Beggar's Opera by John Gay* (Larchmont, New York, 1961), pp. xxv–liv.

E. V. R.

THE BEGGAR'S OPERA

—Nos haec novimus esse nihil.
Mart.

novimus] *O1–2*; novissimus *Q*.

Nos . . . nihil] literally, "We know these things to be nothing," from Martial's *Epigrams*, Book XIII, Poem 2 (entitled "To a Detractor"), line 8. The epigraph is likely to be misconstrued if it is not seen in its original context. In the following prose translation, the epigraph is italicized:

Although you have always a critic's nose, are in a word a nose so great that Atlas on request would not have consented to shoulder it, and though you can deride even Latinus [an actor in pantomime] himself, you cannot say more against my trifling effusions than I have said myself. What pleasure is there in tooth gnawing tooth? You require flesh if you want to be fat. Lest you should waste your time, keep your venom for those that fancy themselves; *I know these efforts of mine are nothing worth.* And yet not altogether nothing if you come to me with a just ear, and not with a morning [i.e., too sober] aspect (Martial, *Epigrams*, trans. Walter C. A. Ker, 3rd printing [New York, 1930], II, 391–393).

DRAMATIS PERSONAE

Men

Peachum		Mr. Hippesley	
Lockit		Mr. Hall	
Macheath		Mr. Walker	
Filch		Mr. Clark	
Jemmy Twitcher	⎫	Mr. H. Bullock	5
Crook-Fingered Jack		Mr. Houghton	
Wat Dreary		Mr. Smith	
Robin of Bagshot	Macheath's Gang	Mr. Lacy	
Nimming Ned		Mr. Pit	
Harry Paddington		Mr. Eaton	10
Matt of the Mint		Mr. Spiller	
Ben Budge	⎭	Mr. Morgan	
Beggar		Mr. Chapman	
Player		Mr. Milward	
	Constables, Drawer, Turnkey, etc.		15

Women

Mrs. Peachum	Mrs. Martin
Polly Peachum	Miss Fenton
Lucy Lockit	Mrs. Egleton
Diana Trapes (slattern)	Mrs. Martin

1. *Peachum*] i.e., "peach them." *Peach* was colloquial for *impeach*, "to accuse and prosecute for Felony and Treason" (Bailey).

3. *Macheath*] i.e., "son of the heath."

5. *Twitcher*] from *to twitch*, "to pinch or pluck" (Bailey); a twitcher was hence a pickpocket or shoplifter.

8. *Bagshot*] Bagshot Heath in northwest Surrey, twenty-six miles from London, was a place of frequent highway robberies (Lives, p. 88).

9. *Nimming*] To *nim* was "to steal or pilfer" (Grose).

10. *Paddington*] A *pad* meant either a highway or a highwayman. A *footpad* was also a highwayman. Since Tyburn was in the parish of Paddington, a hanging day was called "Paddington Fair Day" (Grose).

11. *Mint*] The Mint was a district in Southwark which was originally a sanctuary for debtors but in practice was a sanctuary for all outlaws. Two of the most famous criminal residents of the Mint were Jonathan Wild and Jack Sheppard (Thornbury, VI, 62 f.). See also note to III.vi.24.

12. *Budge*] "one that slips into a house in the dark and steals cloaks, coats, or what comes next to hand"; a *sneaking budge* was "one that robs alone" (Smith).

MRS. COAXER	Mrs. *Holiday*	20
DOLLY TRULL (Prostitute)	Mrs. *Lacy*	
MRS. VIXEN	Mrs. *Rice*	
BETTY DOXY ( )	Women of the Town	Mrs. *Rogers*	
JENNY DIVER *pick pocket*	Mrs. *Clarke*	
MRS. SLAMMEKIN	Mrs. *Morgan*	25
SUKY TAWDRY	Mrs. *Palin*	
MOLLY BRAZEN	Mrs. *Sallee*	

24. *Diver*] "a pickpocket; also one who lives in a cellar" (Grose).

25. *Slammekin*] "a female sloven, one whose clothes seem hung on with a pitch-fork, a careless trapes" (Grose).

The Beggar's Opera

INTRODUCTION

Enter Beggar *and* Player.

BEGGAR.

If poverty be a title to poetry, I am sure nobody can
dispute mine. I own myself of the company of beggars;
and I make one at their weekly festivals at St. Giles's.
I have a small yearly salary for my catches, and am
welcome to a dinner there whenever I please, which is   5
more than most poets can say.

PLAYER.

As we live by the Muses, 'tis but gratitude in us to encourage
poetical merit wherever we find it. The Muses, contrary
to all other ladies, pay no distinction to dress, and never
partially mistake the pertness of embroidery for wit,   10
nor the modesty of want for dulness. Be the author who
he will, we push his play as far as it will go. So (though
you are in want) I wish you success heartily.

BEGGAR.

This piece I own was originally writ for the celebrating
the marriage of James Chanter and Moll Lay, two most   15
excellent ballad-singers. I have introduced the similes
that are in all your celebrated operas: the swallow, the
moth, the bee, the ship, the flower, etc. Besides, I have
a prison scene, which the ladies always reckon charmingly
pathetic. As to the parts, I have observed such a nice   20

---

3. *St. Giles's*] Named after the patron saint of beggars and lepers, the
parish of St. Giles's-in-the-Fields "has passed into a byword as the synonym
of filth and squalor" (Thornbury, III, 206). It was a notorious haunt of
beggars, thieves, and prostitutes. Hogarth portrayed a scene in St. Giles's
in his *Gin Lane.*

−5−

impartiality to our two ladies that it is impossible for either of them to take offense. I hope I may be forgiven, that I have not made my opera throughout unnatural, like those in vogue; for I have no recitative. Excepting this, as I have consented to have neither prologue nor epilogue, 25 it must be allowed an opera in all its forms. The piece indeed hath been heretofore frequently represented by ourselves in our great room at St. Giles's, so that I cannot too often acknowledge your charity in bringing it now on the stage. 30

PLAYER.

But I see 'tis time for us to withdraw; the actors are preparing to begin. Play away the overture. *Exeunt.*

[I.i]　　　　　　*Scene, Peachum's house.*
Peachum *sitting at a table with a large book
of accounts before him.*

AIR I, *An Old Woman Clothed in Gray, etc.*

PEACHUM. Through all the employments of life
　　　　Each neighbor abuses his brother;
　　　　Whore and rogue they call husband and wife;
　　　　All professions be-rogue one another.
　　　　The priest calls the lawyer a cheat;　　　　5
　　　　The lawyer be-knaves the divine;
　　　　And the statesman, because he's so great,
　　　　Thinks his trade as honest as mine.

A lawyer is an honest employment; so is mine. Like me too he acts in a double capacity, both against rogues and for 10

0.4. etc.] *O1–2; om. Q.*

---

21. *our two ladies*] The two leading divas of the Italian opera, Faustina and Cuzzoni, had quarreled publicly to the vast delight of those who disliked opera (Bronson, pp. 207–211).
[I.i]
10. *he . . . capacity*] Like Jonathan Wild, Peachum is a professional criminal, an organizer, who operates both outside the law and within it. He trains young criminals in the arts of robbery and theft, and has a standing arrangement with the gang of highwaymen to purchase stolen goods from them. He makes his profit either by returning the goods to the original owner for a reward (see I.viii.111–118) or by selling them to the public (see III.v.1–18). If he sees that a particular thief is not productive, he can make money by arresting him for a forty-pound reward according to the

'em; for 'tis but fitting that we should protect and encourage cheats, since we live by them.

[I.ii]   Peachum. [*To him enter*] Filch.

(omit)

FILCH.

Sir, Black Moll hath sent word her trial comes on in the afternoon, and she hopes you will order matters so as to bring her off.

PEACHUM.

Why, she may plead her belly at worst; to my knowledge she hath taken care of that security. But as the wench is very   5
active and industrious, you may satisfy her that I'll soften the evidence.

FILCH.

Tom Gagg, sir, is found guilty.

PEACHUM.

A lazy dog! When I took him the time before, I told him what he would come to if he did not mend his hand. This   10
is death without reprieve. I may venture to book him. (*Writes.*) "For Tom Gagg, forty pounds." —Let Betty Sly know that I'll save her from transportation, for I can get more by her staying in England.

[I.i]
12. them] *O1–2*; 'em *Q*.

"Highwayman Act" of 1692 (statutes of 4 and 5 Wm. & Mary, C.8; amended in 6 Geo. I, C. 23), and by persuading other gang members to give false evidence. Though the gang theoretically can reciprocate against him (see III.xiv.11–15), the members do not readily do so because they need him to make their own crime profitable (II.ii.28–36). Then, too, Peachum can reward thieves who are faithful and profitable to him by arranging alibis (softening the evidence) if they are arrested and tried (III.xi.31–33). Once in the gang, a thief, even if he wants to turn honest, is virtually Peachum's slave (I.iii.20–22). Peachum is truly the chief executive of the underworld.

[I.ii]
4. *plead her belly*] a plea of pregnancy, "which a woman capitally convicted may plea in stay of execution; for this, though it is no stay of judgment, yet operates as a respite of execution until she is delivered" (Black). In practice, however, many convicted women escaped hanging because of this plea.

13. *transportation*] a sentence of exile to American and West Indian plantations for a seven or fourteen year period, usually reserved for first offenders found guilty of non-capital crimes (Edward Jenks, *A Short History of English Law* [Boston, 1912], pp. 157, 337).

or Australia

FILCH.

Betty hath brought more goods into our lock to-year than   15
any five of the gang; and in truth, 'tis a pity to lose so good
a customer.

PEACHUM.

If none of the gang take her off, she may, in the common
course of business, live a twelvemonth longer. I love to
let women scape. A good sportsman always lets the hen   20
partridges fly, because the breed of the game depends upon
them. Besides, here the law allows us no reward; there is
nothing to be got by the death of women, except our
wives.

FILCH.

Without dispute, she is a fine woman. 'Twas to her I was   25
obliged for my education, and (to say a bold word) she
hath trained up more young fellows to the business than
the gaming table.

PEACHUM.

Truly, Filch, thy observation is right. We and the
surgeons are more beholden to women than all the pro-   30
fessions besides.

AIR II, *The Bonny Gray-Eyed Morn, etc.*

FILCH.

'Tis woman that seduces all mankind,
  By her we first were taught the wheedling arts;
Her very eyes can cheat; when most she's kind,
  She tricks us of our money with our hearts.   35
  For her, like wolves by night, we roam for prey,

---

15. *lock*] "A cant word, signifying a warehouse where stolen goods are
deposited" (Gay's note to III.iii.15). A *lock* was also "a buyer of stolen
goods" (Grose).

27. *trained . . . business*] In order to support a prostitute like Betty Sly, a
young man like Filch would need more money than he could get honestly;
he would then turn to crime and hence, in order to sell stolen goods, into
"business" with the gang. "Edgworth Bess," for example, corrupted Jack
Sheppard in this way (*Newgate Calendar*, pp. 110 f.).

30. *surgeons . . . women*] Surgeons (i.e., doctors) would receive money for
treating both female complaints and venereal diseases, and would also
receive the bodies of hanged criminals (who were originally corrupted in
order to support prostitutes) for dissection.

And practice ev'ry fraud to bribe her charms;
For suits of love, like law, are won by pay,
And beauty must be fee'd into our arms.

omit?

PEACHUM.

But make haste to Newgate, boy, and let my friends know   40
what I intend; for I love to make them easy one way or
other.

FILCH.

When a gentleman is long kept in suspense, penitence may
break his spirit ever after. Besides, certainty gives a
man a good air upon his trial, and makes him risk another   45
without fear or scruple. But I'll away, for 'tis a pleasure
to be the messenger of comfort to friends in affliction.   [*Exit.*]

pious language

[I.iii]   Peachum [*alone*].

PEACHUM.

But 'tis now high time to look about me for a decent
execution against next sessions. I hate a lazy rogue, by
whom one can get nothing till he is hanged. A register
of the gang. (*Reading.*) "Crook-fingered Jack." A year
and a half in the service. Let me see how much the stock   5
owes to his industry: one, two, three, four, five gold
watches, and seven silver ones. A mighty clean-handed
fellow! Sixteen snuffboxes, five of them of true gold.
Six dozen of handkerchiefs, four silver-hilted swords, half
a dozen of shirts, three tie-periwigs, and a piece of   10
broadcloth. Considering these are only the fruits of his
leisure hours, I don't know a prettier fellow, for no man
alive hath a more engaging presence of mind upon the road.
—"Wat Dreary, alias Brown Will," an irregular dog, who
hath an underhand way of disposing of his goods. I'll try   15
him only for a sessions or two longer upon his good behavior.

---

2. *sessions*] sessions or assizes of criminal court, held eight times each year
at the Old Bailey.

11–12. *fruits . . . hours*] Quite often, criminals worked at honest occupa-
tions during the day, and then robbed at night. Sometimes the jobs were
seasonal, leaving criminals off-season time to commit thefts and robberies.

15. *underhand way*] That is, Wat Dreary is selling his goods to someone
other than Peachum.

—"Harry Paddington," a poor petty-larceny rascal, without the least genius; that fellow, though he were to live these six months, will never come to the gallows with any credit. —"Slippery Sam"; he goes off the next sessions, for 20 the villain hath the impudence to have views of following his trade as a tailor, which he calls an honest employment. —"Matt of the Mint"; listed not above a month ago, a promising sturdy fellow, and diligent in his way; somewhat too bold and hasty, and may raise good contributions on the 25 public, if he does not cut himself short by murder. —"Tom Tipple," a guzzling, soaking sot, who is always too drunk to stand himself, or to make others stand. A cart is absolutely necessary for him. —"Robin of Bagshot, alias Gorgon, alias Bluff Bob, alias Carbuncle, alias Bob Booty." 30

[I.iv]   Peachum. [*To him enter*] Mrs. Peachum.

MRS. PEACHUM.

What of Bob Booty, husband? I hope nothing bad hath betided him. You know, my dear, he's a favorite customer of mine. 'Twas he made me a present of this ring.

PEACHUM.

I have set his name down in the black-list, that's all, my dear; he spends his life among women, and as soon as his 5 money is gone, one or other of the ladies will hang him for the reward, and there's forty pound lost to us forever.

MRS. PEACHUM.

You know, my dear, I never meddle in matters of death; I always leave those affairs to you. Women indeed are bitter bad judges in these cases, for they are so partial to the 10 brave that they think every man handsome who is going to the camp or the gallows.

AIR III, *Cold and Raw, etc.*

If any wench Venus's girdle wear,
   Though she be never so ugly,
Lilies and roses will quickly appear, 15
   And her face look wondrous smugly.

---

30. *Carbuncle*] "a Plague-sore" (Bailey).

Beneath the left ear so fit but a cord
  (A rope so charming a zone is!),
The youth in his cart hath the air of a lord,
  And we cry, "There dies an Adonis!"   20

But really, husband, you should not be too hardhearted, for
you never had a finer, braver set of men than at present.
We have not had a murder among them all, these seven
months. And truly, my dear, that is a great blessing.

PEACHUM.

What a dickens is the woman always a-whimpering about   25
murder for? No gentleman is ever looked upon the worse
for killing a man in his own defense; and if business cannot
be carried on without it, what would you have a gentleman
do?

MRS. PEACHUM.

If I am in the wrong, my dear, you must excuse me,   30
for nobody can help the frailty of an overscrupulous
conscience.

PEACHUM.

Murder is as fashionable a crime as a man can be guilty
of. How many fine gentlemen have we in Newgate every
year, purely upon that article? If they have wherewithal 35
to persuade the jury to bring it in manslaughter, what
are they the worse for it? So, my dear, have done upon
this subject. Was Captain Macheath here this morning, for
the bank notes he left with you last week?

MRS. PEACHUM.

Yes, my dear; and though the bank hath stopped payment, 40
he was so cheerful and so agreeable! Sure there is not

---

20. *Adonis*] "the fair son of *Cynaras*, King of *Cyprus*, who being killed by a
wild Boar, was changed into a purple flower by *Venus* . . ." (Bailey).

36. *manslaughter*] Such a case was described in 1710 by Zacharias Conrad
von Uffenbach (*London in 1710, From the Travels of Zacharias Conrad von
Uffenbach*, ed. W. H. Quarrell and Margaret Mare [London, 1934], pp.
125 f.).

39–40. *bank notes . . . payment*] Bank notes, or bank bills, were actually
receipts for money deposited, but in circulation were similar to cashier's
checks today. Because they were made payable to the bearer, however,
thieves could cash them if they moved rapidly before stop-payment notice
was sent to the bank on which they were drawn. By demanding payment,

a finer gentleman upon the road than the Captain! If
he comes from Bagshot at any reasonable hour he hath
promised to make one this evening with Polly, and me, and
Bob Booty, at a party of quadrille. Pray, my dear, is the   45
Captain rich?

PEACHUM.

The Captain keeps too good company ever to grow rich.
Marybone and the chocolate houses are his undoing. The
man that proposes to get money by play should have the
education of a fine gentleman, and be trained up to it   50
from his youth.

MRS. PEACHUM.

Really, I am sorry upon Polly's account the Captain hath
not more discretion. What business hath he to keep company
with lords and gentlemen? He should leave them to prey
upon one another.   55

PEACHUM.

"Upon Polly's account!" What a plague does the woman
mean? "Upon Polly's account!"

MRS. PEACHUM.

Captain Macheath is very fond of the girl.

PEACHUM.

And what then?

MRS. PEACHUM.

If I have any skill in the ways of women, I am sure Polly   60
thinks him a very pretty man.

---

the thief or his agent would also necessarily identify himself as an illegal
possessor (see III.iv.39–40). In 1738 the banks began issuing bank bills
payable at "seven days' sight," so that a thief would have to wait seven
days before receiving payment—ample time for the victim to request stop
payment and for a criminal trying to cash the bills to be apprehended
(Thornbury, I, 460 f.).

45. *quadrille*] a card game, "a four-handed French variation of ombre,"
that was the latest fashion in 1728 (Henry Fielding, *The Author's Farce*, ed.
Charles B. Woods [Lincoln, Nebr., 1966], p. 49, note to III.217).

48. *Marybone*] also Marrowbone, now Marylebone. Marybone Gardens
was situated about three-fourths of a mile north of Tyburn. The famous
bowling green there prompted a good deal of gambling and side-betting.

48. *chocolate houses*] Dice and cards were the implements of gambling
at the numerous chocolate houses, so named because hot cocoa was also
obtainable. A scene at a gambling table in White's Chocolate House is
shown in Plate 6 of Hogarth's *Rake's Progress*.

PEACHUM.

And what then? You would not be so mad to have the wench
marry him. Gamesters and highwaymen are generally very
good to their whores, but they are very devils to their wives.

MRS. PEACHUM.

But if Polly should be in love, how should we help her, or   65
how can she help herself? Poor girl, I am in the utmost
concern about her.

AIR IV, *Why is Your Faithful Slave Disdained?* etc.

If love the virgin's heart invade,
How, like a moth, the simple maid
Still plays about the flame!   70
If soon she be not made a wife,
Her honor's singed, and then for life,
She's—what I dare not name.

PEACHUM.

Look ye, wife. A handsome wench in our way of business is
as profitable as at the bar of a Temple coffeehouse, who   75
looks upon it as her livelihood to grant every liberty but one.
You see I would indulge the girl as far as prudently we
can—in anything but marriage! After that, my dear, how
shall we be safe? Are we not then in her husband's power?
For a husband hath the absolute power over all a wife's   80
secrets but her own. If the girl had the discretion of a
court lady, who can have a dozen young fellows at her
ear without complying with one, I should not matter it;
but Polly is tinder, and a spark will at once set her on
a flame. Married! If the wench does not know her own   85
profit, sure she knows her own pleasure better than to
make herself a property! My daughter to me should be,

67.1. *etc.*] *O1–2; om. Q.*

---

75. *Temple*] "a famous College of the Students of the Law in *Fleet-street,
London*; formerly the Residence of the Knights Templars in *England*"
(Bailey).

86–87. *to . . . property*] Upon marriage a wife and her possessions became
the husband's legal property.

87–89. *My daughter . . . gang*] Compare with IV.vi of *Gulliver's Travels*:
"THERE are three Methods by which a Man may rise to be Chief Minister:
The first is, by knowing how with Prudence to dispose of a Wife, a Daughter,
or a Sister . . ." (*Gulliver's Travels, 1726*, intro. by Harold Williams [*The*

like a court lady to a minister of state, a key to the whole gang. Married! If the affair is not already done, I'll terrify her from it, by the example of our neighbors. 90

MRS. PEACHUM.

Mayhap, my dear, you may injure the girl. She loves to imitate the fine ladies, and she may only allow the Captain liberties in the view of interest.

PEACHUM.

But 'tis your duty, my dear, to warn the girl against her ruin, and to instruct her how to make the most of her 95 beauty. I'll go to her this moment, and sift her. In the meantime, wife, rip out the coronets and marks of these dozen of cambric handkerchiefs, for I can dispose of them this afternoon to a chap in the City. [*Exit.*]

[I.v] Mrs. Peachum [*alone*].

MRS. PEACHUM.

Never was a man more out of the way in an argument than my husband. Why must our Polly, forsooth, differ from her sex, and love only her husband? And why must Polly's marriage, contrary to all observation, make her the less followed by other men? All men are thieves in love, and 5 like a woman the better for being another's property.

AIR V, *Of All the Simple Things We Do, etc.*

A maid is like the golden ore,
Which hath guineas intrinsical in't,
Whose worth is never known before
It is tried and impressed in the mint. 10
A wife's like a guinea in gold,
Stamped with the name of her spouse,

7. ore] *NC*; oar *O1–2, Q.*

Prose Works of Jonathan Swift, ed. Herbert Davis, Vol. XI, Oxford, 1941], p. 239).

98. *cambric*] "a sort of fine Linnen Cloth brought from *Cambray* in *Flanders*" (Bailey). Cambric was in great demand in 1729, according to Joshua Gee (pp. 15, 34, 116).

99. *chap*] "in Commerce, a Chapman, or Customer" (Bailey).

99. *the City*] "a large walled Town" (Bailey), specifically the original precincts of London within the walls.

Now here, now there, is bought, or is sold,
And is current in every house.   = currency

[I.vi]   Mrs. Peachum. [*To her enter*] Filch.

MRS. PEACHUM.   omit

Come hither, Filch. I am as fond of this child as though
my mind misgave me he were my own. He hath as fine
a hand at picking a pocket as a woman, and is as nimble-
fingered as a juggler. If an unlucky session does not cut
the rope of thy life, I pronounce, boy, thou wilt be a   5
great man in history. Where was your post last night, my
boy?

FILCH.

I plied at the opera, madam; and considering 'twas neither
dark nor rainy, so that there was no great hurry in getting
chairs and coaches, made a tolerable hand on't. These   10
seven handkerchiefs, madam.

MRS. PEACHUM.

Colored ones, I see. They are of sure sale from our warehouse
at Redriff among the seamen.

FILCH.

And this snuffbox.

MRS. PEACHUM.

Set in gold! A pretty encouragement this to a young   15
beginner.

FILCH.

I had a fair tug at a charming gold watch. Pox take the
tailors for making the fobs so deep and narrow! It stuck
by the way, and I was forced to make my escape under a
coach. Really, madam, I fear I shall be cut off in the   20
flower of my youth, so that every now and then (since I was
pumped) I have thoughts of taking up and going to sea.
discipline

13. *Redriff*] Rotherhithe, the port district of London on the south bank
of the Thames about a mile east of the Tower. The common name *Redriff*
(used by Gulliver) was replaced by the written form *Rotherhithe* during the
eighteenth century.
22. *pumped*] Placing an offender under a water pump was "a piece of
discipline administered to a pickpocket caught in the fact, when there is no
pond at hand" (Grose). This punishment was intended to scare youthful
offenders away from crime by making them feel the pain of drowning. The

MRS. PEACHUM.

You should go to Hockley in the Hole, and to Marybone,
child, to learn valor. These are the schools that have
bred so many brave men. I thought, boy, by this time,   25
thou hadst lost fear as well as shame. Poor lad! How little
does he know as yet of the Old Bailey. For the first fact
I'll insure thee from being hanged; and going to sea,
Filch, will come time enough upon a sentence of transportation. But now, since you have nothing better to   30
do, ev'n go to your book, and learn your catechism; for
really a man makes but an ill figure in the Ordinary's
paper, who cannot give a satisfactory answer to his
questions. But, hark you, my lad. Don't tell me a lie, for
you know I hate a liar. Do you know of anything that   35
hath passed between Captain Macheath and our Polly?

FILCH.

I beg you, madam, don't ask me; for I must either tell a
lie to you or to Miss Polly; for I promised her I would not
tell.

MRS. PEACHUM.

But when the honor of our family is concerned—   40

FILCH.

I shall lead a sad life with Miss Polly if ever she come to

---

next time a youth like Filch was caught and recognized, he would likely be
arrested and arraigned, then transported.

23. *Hockley in the Hole*] or Hockley Hole. Near Clerkenwell Green,
Hockley in the Hole was notorious as a place of bear and bull baiting,
sword fighting, wrestling, and dog fighting. It was synonymous with
vulgarity and brutality (Thornbury, II, 306). It is now Ray Street and that
part of Farringdon Road between Ray Street and Clerkenwell Road.

31–34. *learn . . . questions*] i.e., Filch, as an apprentice thief, should
study his catechism so that he may, upon his first arraignment at the Old
Bailey, satisfy the requirements of "Benefit of Clergy" for first offenders.
According to this provision, which was rooted in ecclesiastical law, a felon
able to read a required passage of scripture (usually the first verse of
Psalm 51, which was popularly called either the "neck verse" or
"hanging verse") could escape the death penalty and receive the lighter
sentence of transportation. The ordinary of Newgate (i.e., an ordained
minister, a chaplain) would ask the prisoner to read the passage, and then
would declare to the judge whether benefit of clergy should be given. The
thief who knew his catechism could thus pass the test and gain a light
sentence.

know that I told you. Besides, I would not willingly forfeit
my own honor by betraying anybody.

MRS. PEACHUM.

Yonder comes my husband and Polly. Come, Filch, you
shall go with me into my own room, and tell me the whole   45
story. I'll give thee a glass of a most delicious cordial
that I keep for my own drinking.   [*Exeunt.*]

[I.vii]   [*Enter*] Peachum [*and*] Polly.

POLLY.

I know as well as any of the fine ladies how to make the
most of myself and of my man too. A woman knows how to
be mercenary, though she hath never been in a court or at
an assembly. We have it in our natures, Papa. If I allow
Captain Macheath some trifling liberties, I have this   5
watch and other visible marks of his favor to show for it.
A girl who cannot grant some things, and refuse what is
most material, will make but a poor hand of her beauty,
and soon be thrown upon the common.

AIR VI, *What Shall I Do to Show How Much I Love Her, etc.*

Virgins are like the fair flower in its luster,   10
  Which in the garden enamels the ground;
Near it the bees in play flutter and cluster,
  And gaudy butterflies frolic around.
But, when once plucked, 'tis no longer alluring,
  To Covent Garden 'tis sent (as yet sweet),   15
There fades, and shrinks, and grows past all enduring,
  Rots, stinks, and dies, and is trod under feet.

PEACHUM.

You know, Polly, I am not against your toying and trifling
with a customer in the way of business, or to get out a
secret, or so. But if I find out that you have played the   20

46–47. glass . . . cordial] *O2, Q*;
most delicious glass of a cordial *O1.*

---

9. *common*] a pun, (1) common land, (2) common law.
15. *Covent Garden*] London's central market place for produce, and also
an area plied by prostitutes.

fool and are married, you jade you, I'll cut your throat, hussy. Now you know my mind.

[I.viii]   Peachum, Polly. [*Enter to them*] Mrs. Peachum.

AIR VII, *Oh London Is a Fine Town*

MRS. PEACHUM (*in a very great passion*).

Our Polly is a sad slut, nor heeds what we have
    taught her.
I wonder any man alive will ever rear a daughter!
For she must have both hoods and gowns, and hoops
    to swell her pride,
With scarfs and stays, and gloves and lace; and she will
    have men beside;
And when she's dressed with care and cost, all-tempting,
    fine and gay,   5
As men should serve a cowcumber, she flings herself away.
    Our Polly is a sad slut, etc.

You baggage! You hussy! You inconsiderate jade! Had you
been hanged, it would not have vexed me, for that might
have been your misfortune; but to do such a mad thing by   10
choice! The wench is married, husband.

PEACHUM.

Married! The Captain is a bold man, and will risk anything
for money; to be sure he believes her a fortune. Do you
think your mother and I should have lived comfortably so
long together, if ever we had been married? Baggage!   15

MRS. PEACHUM.

I knew she was always a proud slut; and now the wench
hath played the fool and married, because forsooth she
would do like the gentry. Can you support the expense
of a husband, hussy, in gaming, drinking, and whoring?
Have you money enough to carry on the daily quarrels of   20
man and wife about who shall squander most? There are

7. Our Polly...etc.] *O1–2; om. Q*

---

6. *As men ... cowcumber*] Cucumbers were often thought to be poisonous, and thus should be served by being thrown away (Robert S. Hunting, "How Much is a Cowcumber Worth?" *N & Q*, CXCVIII [1953], 28 f.).

7. Our Polly ... etc.] The first two lines of the song are to be repeated.

not many husbands and wives who can bear the charges of
plaguing one another in a handsome way. If you must be
married, could you introduce nobody into our family but
a highwayman? Why, thou foolish jade, thou wilt be as   25
ill used, and as much neglected, as if thou hadst married a
lord!

PEACHUM.

Let not your anger, my dear, break through the rules of
decency, for the Captain looks upon himself in the military
capacity, as a gentleman by his profession. Besides what   30
he hath already, I know he is in a fair way of getting, or
of dying; and both these ways, let me tell you, are most
excellent chances for a wife. Tell me, hussy, are you
ruined or no?

MRS. PEACHUM.

With Polly's fortune, she might very well have gone off   35
to a person of distinction. Yes, that you might, you pouting
slut!

PEACHUM.

What, is the wench dumb? Speak, or I'll make you plead by
squeezing out an answer from you. Are you really bound
wife to him, or are you only upon liking?   (*Pinches her.*)   40

POLLY (*screaming*).

Oh!

MRS. PEACHUM.

How the mother is to be pitied who hath handsome
daughters! Locks, bolts, bars, and lectures of morality
are nothing to them; they break through them all. They   45
have as much pleasure in cheating a father and mother
as in cheating at cards.

PEACHUM.

Why, Polly, I shall soon know if you are married, by
Macheath's keeping from our house.

   AIR VIII, *Grim King of the Ghosts, etc.*

POLLY.   Can love be controlled by advice?
          Will Cupid our mothers obey?   50
     Though my heart were as frozen as ice,
          At his flame 'twould have melted away.
     When he kissed me so closely he pressed,

'Twas so sweet that I must have complied;
So I thought it both safest and best　　　　55
To marry, for fear you should chide.

MRS. PEACHUM.

Then all the hopes of our family are gone forever and
ever.

PEACHUM.

And Macheath may hang his father and mother-in-law, in
hope to get into their daughter's fortune.　　　　60

POLLY.

I did not marry him (as 'tis the fashion) coolly and
deliberately for honor or money. But I love him.

MRS. PEACHUM.

Love him! Worse and worse! I thought the girl had been
better bred. Oh husband, husband! Her folly makes me
mad! My head swims! I'm distracted! I can't support　65
myself. —Oh!　　　　　　　　　　　　　　*Faints.*

PEACHUM.

See, wench, to what a condition you have reduced your poor
mother. A glass of cordial, this instant. How the poor
woman takes it to heart.

Polly *goes out, and returns with it.*
[Peachum *helps* Mrs. Peachum *drink.*]

Ah, hussy, now this is the only comfort your mother has left.　70

POLLY.

Give her another glass, sir; my mama drinks double the
quantity whenever she is out of order.

[*He pours;* Mrs. Peachum *drinks.*]

This, you see, fetches her.

MRS. PEACHUM.

The girl shows such a readiness, and so much concern, that
I could almost find in my heart to forgive her.　　　　75

AIR IX, *Oh Jenny, Oh Jenny, Where Hast Thou Been*

Oh Polly, you might have toyed and kissed.
By keeping men off, you keep them on.

POLLY.　　　　　　But he so teased me,
And he so pleased me,
What I did, you must have done.　　　　80

MRS. PEACHUM.

Not with a highwayman. You sorry slut!

PEACHUM.

A word with you, wife. 'Tis no new thing for a wench to take man without consent of parents. You know 'tis the frailty of woman, my dear.

MRS. PEACHUM.

Yes, indeed, the sex is frail. But the first time a woman   85
is frail, she should be somewhat nice methinks, for then or never is the time to make her fortune. After that, she hath nothing to do but to guard herself from being found out, and she may do what she pleases.

PEACHUM.

Make yourself a little easy; I have a thought shall soon set   90
all matters again to rights. [*To* Polly.]   Why so melancholy, Polly? Since what is done cannot be undone, we must all endeavor to make the best of it.

MRS. PEACHUM.

Well, Polly, as far as one woman can forgive another, I forgive thee. Your father is too fond of you, hussy.   95

POLLY.

Then all my sorrows are at an end.

MRS. PEACHUM.

A mighty likely speech in troth, for a wench who is just married!

AIR X, *Thomas, I Cannot, etc.*

POLLY.   I, like a ship in storms, was tossed;
                Yet afraid to put in to land;   100
                For seized in the port the vessel's lost
                Whose treasure is contraband.
                    The waves are laid,
                    My duty's paid.
                Oh joy beyond expression!   105
                    Thus, safe ashore,
                    I ask no more,
                My all is in my possession.

PEACHUM.

I hear customers in t'other room. Go, talk with 'em, Polly, but come to us again as soon as they are gone. 110

But hark ye, child: If 'tis the gentleman who was here
yesterday about the repeating watch, say you believe we
can't get intelligence of it till tomorrow. For I lent it to
Suky Straddle, to make a figure with it tonight at a tavern
in Drury Lane. If t'other gentleman calls for the silver- 115
hilted sword, you know Beetle-Browed Jemmy hath it on;
and he doth not come from Tunbridge till Tuesday night,
so that it cannot be had till then.   [*Exit* Polly.]

[I.ix]   Peachum [*and*] Mrs. Peachum [*remain*].

PEACHUM.

Dear wife, be a little pacified. Don't let your passion
run away with your senses. Polly, I grant you, hath done a
rash thing.

MRS. PEACHUM.

If she had had only an intrigue with the fellow, why the
very best families have excused and huddled up a frailty of   5
that sort. 'Tis marriage, husband, that makes it a blemish.

PEACHUM.

But money, wife, is the true fuller's earth for reputations;
there is not a spot or a stain but what it can take out.
A rich rogue nowadays is fit company for any gentleman;
and the world, my dear, hath not such a contempt for   10
roguery as you imagine. I tell you, wife, I can make this
match turn to our advantage.

MRS. PEACHUM.

I am very sensible, husband, that Captain Macheath is
worth money, but I am in doubt whether he hath not two
or three wives already, and then if he should die in a   15
session or two, Polly's dower would come into dispute.

111–118. *If . . . then*] Victims of robberies frequently advertised that
they would give a reward for stolen possessions. Receivers of stolen goods
would contact the victims and then arrange for a recovery (Fielding, pp.
76–82). Jonathan Wild operated in this way. Peachum, before restoring
the watch and the sword, has given them to gang members, who have
thereby been able to impress people, gain their confidence, and then
commit robberies from the "inside."
117. *Tunbridge*] Tunbridge Wells, a fashionable resort spa, about
thirty-five miles southeast of London.

–22–

PEACHUM.

That, indeed, is a point which ought to be considered.

AIR XI, *A Soldier and a Sailor*

A fox may steal your hens, sir,
A whore your health and pence, sir,
Your daughter rob your chest, sir,   20
Your wife may steal your rest, sir,
    A thief your goods and plate.
But this is all but picking,
With rest, pence, chest, and chicken;
It ever was decreed, sir,   25
If lawyer's hand is fee'd, sir,
    He steals your whole estate.

The lawyers are bitter enemies to those in our way. They
don't care that anybody should get a clandestine livelihood
but themselves.   30

[I.x]   Mrs. Peachum, Peachum. [*To them enter*] Polly.

POLLY.

'Twas only Nimming Ned. He brought in a damask window
curtain, a hoop-petticoat, a pair of silver candlesticks, a
periwig, and one silk stocking, from the fire that happened
last night.

PEACHUM.

There is not a fellow that is cleverer in his way, and saves   5
more goods out of the fire, than Ned. But now, Polly, to
your affair; for matters must not be left as they are. You
are married then, it seems?

POLLY.

Yes, sir.

PEACHUM.

And how do you propose to live, child?   10

POLLY.

Like other women, sir, upon the industry of my husband.

MRS. PEACHUM.

What, is the wench turned fool? A highwayman's wife, like a
soldier's, hath as little of his pay as of his company.

– 23 –

PEACHUM.

And had not you the common views of a gentlewoman in
your marriage, Polly?   15

POLLY.

I don't know what you mean, sir.

PEACHUM.

Of a jointure, and of being a widow.

POLLY.

But I love him, sir. How then could I have thoughts of
parting with him?

PEACHUM.

Parting with him! Why, that is the whole scheme and   20
intention of all marriage articles. The comfortable estate
of widowhood is the only hope that keeps up a wife's
spirits. Where is the woman who would scruple to be a
wife, if she had it in her power to be a widow whenever she
pleased? If you have any views of this sort, Polly, I shall   25
think the match not so very unreasonable.

POLLY.

How I dread to hear your advice! Yet I must beg you to
explain yourself.

PEACHUM.

Secure what he hath got, have him peached the next
sessions, and then at once you are made a rich widow.   30

POLLY.

What, murder the man I love! The blood runs cold at my
heart with the very thought of it.

PEACHUM.

Fie, Polly! What hath murder to do in the affair? Since
the thing sooner or later must happen, I dare say, the
Captain himself would like that we should get the reward   35
for his death sooner than a stranger. Why, Polly, the
Captain knows that as 'tis his employment to rob, so
'tis ours to take robbers. Every man in his business. So that
there is no malice in the case.

MRS. PEACHUM.

Ay, husband, now you have nicked the matter. To have   40

---

17. *jointure*] "a Maintenance allotted or join'd to the Wife, in Consideration of the Dowry she brought her Husband" (Bailey).
40. *nicked*] To *nick* means "to win at dice, to hit the mark just in the nick
of time, or at the critical moment" (Grose).

him peached is the only thing could ever make me forgive her.

AIR XII, *Now Ponder Well, Ye Parents Dear*

POLLY.   Oh, ponder well! Be not severe;
                 So save a wretched wife!
                 For on the rope that hangs my dear   45
                 Depends poor Polly's life.

MRS. PEACHUM.

But your duty to your parents, hussy, obliges you to hang him. What would many a wife give for such an opportunity.

POLLY.

What is a jointure, what is widowhood to me? I know my heart. I cannot survive him.   50

AIR XIII, *Le Printemps Rappelle aux Armes*

The turtle thus with plaintive crying,
    Her lover dying,
The turtle thus with plaintive crying
    Laments her dove.
Down she drops quite spent with sighing   55
Paired in death, as paired in love.

Thus, sir, it will happen to your poor Polly.

MRS. PEACHUM.

What, is the fool in love in earnest then? I hate thee for being particular. Why, wench, thou art a shame to thy very sex.   60

POLLY.

But hear me, mother. If you ever loved—

MRS. PEACHUM.

Those cursed playbooks she reads have been her ruin. One word more, hussy, and I shall knock your brains out, if you have any.

55. spent] *O1-2, Q (some copies);*
pent *Q (some copies).*

---

46. *depends*] a pun, (1) depends, (2) hangs (original Latin meaning). One story has it that this "painful and ridiculous image" together with the "innocent looks of" Lavinia Fenton in singing the song, "saved" the play from the audience's "disposition to damn it" (Schultz, p. 4).

PEACHUM.

Keep out of the way, Polly, for fear of mischief, and consider 65
of what is proposed to you.

MRS. PEACHUM.

Away, hussy. Hang your husband, and be dutiful.

[*Exit* Polly *to a hiding place, in view of the audience, where she can overhear*
Peachum *and* Mrs. Peachum.]

[I.xi]   Mrs. Peachum, Peachum. Polly *listening*.

MRS. PEACHUM.

The thing, husband, must and shall be done. For the sake
of intelligence we must take other measures, and have him
peached the next session without her consent. If she will not
know her duty, we know ours.

PEACHUM.

But really, my dear, it grieves one's heart to take off a   5
great man. When I consider his personal bravery, his fine
stratagem, how much we have already got by him, and how
much more we may get, methinks I can't find in my heart
to have a hand in his death. I wish you could have made
Polly undertake it.   10

MRS. PEACHUM.

But in a case of necessity—our own lives are in danger.

PEACHUM.

Then, indeed, we must comply with the customs of the
world, and make gratitude give way to interest. He shall
be taken off.

MRS. PEACHUM.

I'll undertake to manage Polly.   15

PEACHUM.

And I'll prepare matters for the Old Bailey.   [*Exeunt.*]

[I.xii]   Polly [*alone*].

POLLY.

Now I'm a wretch, indeed. Methinks I see him already in
the cart, sweeter and more lovely than the nosegay in his
hand. I hear the crowd extolling his resolution and

---

7. *stratagem*] "a politick Device, or subtil Invention in War" (Bailey).

intrepidity. What volleys of sighs are sent from the windows
of Holborn, that so comely a youth should be brought to   5
disgrace. I see him at the tree! The whole circle are in
tears! Even butchers weep! Jack Ketch himself hesitates
to perform his duty, and would be glad to lose his fee by
a reprieve. What then will become of Polly? —As yet I
may inform him of their design, and aid him in his escape.   10
It shall be so. But then he flies, absents himself, and I
bar myself from his dear, dear conversation. That too
will distract me. If he keep out of the way, my papa and
mama may in time relent, and we may be happy. If he
stays, he is hanged, and then he is lost forever! He intended   15
to lie concealed in my room till the dusk of the evening. If
they are abroad, I'll this instant let him out, lest some
accident should prevent him.   *Exit, and returns* [*with* Macheath.]

[I.xiii]   Polly, Macheath.

                                  AIR XIV, *Pretty Parrot, Say*

MACHEATH.   Pretty Polly, say,
                                  When I was away,
                                  Did your fancy never stray
                                  To some newer lover?
POLLY.   Without disguise,   5
                                  Heaving sighs,
                                  Doting eyes,
                                  My constant heart discover.
                                  Fondly let me loll!
MACHEATH.   Oh pretty, pretty Poll.   10
POLLY.

And are you as fond as ever, my dear?

0.2. *Say*] *O1–2*; say, etc. *Q*.

_____

[I.xii]
  5. *Holborn*] a part of the way from Newgate to Tyburn Tree. Condemned
criminals, nooses around their necks, rode backwards along the way in a
cart, frequently with their coffins; the spectacle brought out throngs of
spectators. A hanging at Tyburn is portrayed by Hogarth in *Industry and
Idleness*, Plate XI.
  7. *Jack Ketch*] the symbolic name for the hangman, and apparently a
corruption of the name Richard *Jaquett*, who was hangman in the 1670's
(Thornbury, V, 196).

MACHEATH.

Suspect my honor, my courage, suspect anything but my love. May my pistols miss fire, and my mare slip her shoulder while I am pursued, if I ever forsake thee.

POLLY.

Nay, my dear, I have no reason to doubt you, for I find in the romance you lent me, none of the great heroes were ever false in love. 15

AIR XV, *Pray, Fair One, Be Kind*

MACHEATH.

My heart was so free,
It roved like the bee,
Till Polly my passion requited; 20
I sipped each flower,
I changed ev'ry hour,
But here ev'ry flower is united.

POLLY.

Were you sentenced to transportation, sure, my dear, you could not leave me behind you, could you? 25

MACHEATH.

Is there any power, any force that could tear me from thee?
You might sooner tear a pension out of the hands of a courtier, a fee from a lawyer, a pretty woman from a looking glass, or any woman from quadrille. But to tear me from thee is impossible. 30

AIR XVI, *Over the Hills and Far Away*

Were I laid on Greenland's coast,
And in my arms embraced my lass,
Warm amidst eternal frost,
Too soon the half year's night would pass.

POLLY.

Were I sold on Indian soil 35
Soon as the burning day was closed,
I could mock the sultry toil,
When on my charmer's breast reposed.

MACHEATH. And I would love you all the day,
POLLY. Every night would kiss and play, 40
MACHEATH. If with me you'd fondly stray
POLLY. Over the hills and far away.

POLLY.

Yes, I would go with thee. But oh, how shall I speak it?
I must be torn from thee. We must part.

MACHEATH.

How? Part?   45

POLLY.

We must, we must. My papa and mama are set against
thy life. They now, even now, are in search after thee.
They are preparing evidence against thee. Thy life depends
upon a moment.

AIR XVII *(Gin Thou Wert Mine Awn Thing*

Oh what pain it is to part!   50
  Can I leave thee, can I leave thee?
Oh what pain it is to part!
  Can thy Polly ever leave thee?
But lest death my love should thwart,
And bring thee to the fatal cart,   55
Thus I tear thee from my bleeding heart!
  Fly hence, and let me leave thee.

One kiss and then—one kiss—begone—farewell.

MACHEATH.

My hand, my heart, my dear, is so riveted to thine, that
I cannot unloose my hold.   60

POLLY.

But my papa may intercept thee, and then I should lose
the very glimmering of hope. A few weeks, perhaps, may
reconcile us all. Shall thy Polly hear from thee?

MACHEATH.

Must I then go?

POLLY.

And will not absence change your love?   65

MACHEATH.

If you doubt it, let me stay, and be hanged.

POLLY.

Oh how I fear! How I tremble! Go, but when safety will
give you leave, you will be sure to see me again; for till
then Polly is wretched.

[*During the following song,* Polly *and* Macheath *are*] *parting, and looking
back at each other with fondness; he at one door, she at the other.*

AIR XVIII, *Oh, the Broom, etc.*

MACHEATH.

The miser thus a shilling sees,　　　　　70
　　Which he's obliged to pay,
With sighs resigns it by degrees,
　　And fears 'tis gone for aye.

POLLY.

The boy thus, when his sparrow's flown,
　　The bird in silence eyes;　　　　75
But soon as out of sight 'tis gone,
　　Whines, whimpers, sobs, and cries.　　　[*Exeunt.*]

[*End of the First Act.*]

ACT II

A tavern near Newgate.

Jemmy Twitcher, Crook-Fingered Jack, Wat Dreary, Robin of
Bagshot, Nimming Ned, Henry Paddington, Matt of the Mint,
Ben Budge, *and the rest of the gang, at the table, with wine, brandy, and
tobacco.*

BEN BUDGE.

But prithee, Matt, what is become of thy brother Tom? I
have not seen him since my return from transportation.

MATT OF THE MINT.

Poor brother Tom had an accident this time twelvemonth,
and so clever a made fellow he was, that I could not save him
from those flaying rascals the surgeons; and now, poor   5
man, he is among the ottomies at Surgeon's Hall.

BEN BUDGE.

So it seems his time was come.

JEMMY TWITCHER.

But the present time is ours, and nobody alive hath more.
Why are the laws leveled at us? Are we more dishonest
than the rest of mankind? What we win, gentlemen, is our   10
own by the law of arms and the right of conquest.

CROOK-FINGERED JACK.

Where shall we find such another set of practical philos-
ophers, who to a man are above the fear of death?

WAT DREARY.

Sound men, and true!

ROBIN OF BAGSHOT.

Of tried courage and indefatigable industry!   15

NIMMING NED.

Who is there here that would not die for his friend?

3–6. *Poor . . . Hall*] Though usually a relative could claim the body of a
hanged criminal, Matt has been unsuccessful. His brother Tom was taken
to the Barber Surgeons Hall in Monkwell Street, where surgeons performed
a dissection for instructional purposes. After the dissection, Tom's skeleton
(*ottomy*, from *anatomy, anatomize*) was put on display. For a scene of a
dissection in the Barber Surgeons Theater, and a display of "ottomies,"
see Plate IV of Hogarth's *Four Stages of Cruelty*. The form *ottomies* is from
Grose; Gay has *otamys.*

HENRY PADDINGTON.

Who is there here that would betray him for his interest?

MATT OF THE MINT.

Show me a gang of courtiers that can say as much.

BEN BUDGE.

We are for a just partition of the world, for every man
hath a right to enjoy life.   20

MATT OF THE MINT.

We retrench the superfluities of mankind. The world is
avaricious, and I hate avarice. A covetous fellow, like
a jackdaw, steals what he was never made to enjoy, for the
sake of hiding it. These are the robbers of mankind, for
money was made for the freehearted and generous, and   25
where is the injury of taking from another what he hath not
the heart to make use of?

JEMMY TWITCHER.

Our several stations for the day are fixed. Good luck
attend us all. Fill the glasses.

AIR XIX, *Fill Ev'ry Glass, etc.*

MATT OF THE MINT.

> Fill ev'ry glass, for wine inspires us,   30
>   And fires us
> With courage, love, and joy.
> Women and wine should life employ.
> Is there aught else on earth desirous?

CHORUS.

> Fill ev'ry glass, etc.   35

[II.ii]   *To them enter* Macheath.

MACHEATH.

Gentlemen, well met. My heart hath been with you this
hour; but an unexpected affair hath detained me. No
ceremony, I beg you.

29.1. AIR XIX] *O2, Q*; AIR I *O1*.   *to act. This different numbering in O1*
In O1, all songs are numbered according   *will not subsequently be noted.*

---

23. *jackdaw*] The jackdaw, a bird of the pie kind, was popularly thought
to be one of "the veriest thieves . . . especially for silver and gold" (*OED*).

MATT OF THE MINT.

We were just breaking up to go upon duty. Am I to have
the honor of taking the air with you, sir, this evening   5
upon the heath? I drink a dram now and then with the
stagecoachmen in the way of friendship and intelligence;
and I know that about this time there will be passengers
upon the western road who are worth speaking with.

MACHEATH.

I was to have been of that party, but—   10

MATT OF THE MINT.

But what, sir?

MACHEATH.

Is there any man who suspects my courage?

MATT OF THE MINT.

We have all been witnesses of it.

MACHEATH.

My honor and truth to the gang?

MATT OF THE MINT.

I'll be answerable for it.   15

MACHEATH.

In the division of our booty, have I ever shown the least
marks of avarice or injustice?

MATT OF THE MINT.

By these questions something seems to have ruffled you.
Are any of us suspected?

MACHEATH.

I have a fixed confidence, gentlemen, in you all, as men of   20
honor, and as such I value and respect you. Peachum is a
man that is useful to us.

MATT OF THE MINT.

Is he about to play us any foul play? I'll shoot him through
the head.

MACHEATH.

I beg you, gentlemen, act with conduct and discretion. A   25
pistol is your last resort.

MATT OF THE MINT.

He knows nothing of this meeting.

MACHEATH.

Business cannot go on without him. He is a man who knows

the world, and is a necessary agent to us. We have had a
slight difference, and till it is accommodated I shall be   30
obliged to keep out of his way. Any private dispute of
mine shall be of no ill consequence to my friends. You
must continue to act under his direction, for the moment
we break loose from him, our gang is ruined.

MATT OF THE MINT.

As a bawd to a whore, I grant you, he is to us of great   35
convenience.

MACHEATH.

Make him believe I have quitted the gang, which I can
never do but with life. At our private quarters I will continue
to meet you. A week or so will probably reconcile us.

MATT OF THE MINT.

Your instructions shall be observed. 'Tis now high time   40
for us to repair to our several duties; so till the evening
at our quarters in Moorfields, we bid you farewell.

MACHEATH.

I shall wish myself with you. Success attend you.

Sits down melancholy at the table.

AIR XX, *March in "Rinaldo," with Drums and Trumpets*

MATT OF THE MINT.

Let us take the road.
Hark! I hear the sound of coaches!   45
The hour of attack approaches,
To your arms, brave boys, and load.
See the ball I hold!   [*Holding up bullet.*]
Let the chymists toil like asses,
Our fire their fire surpasses,   50
And turns all our lead to gold.

*The gang, ranged in the front of the stage, load their pistols, and stick them
under their girdles; then go off singing the first part in chorus.*

---

42. *Moorfields*] Frequented by many criminals, Moorfields was a place of
brandy shops, hangouts, and fields for cudgel-playing, wrestling, quoits,
etc. In 1735 it was claimed that Moorfields had "ruined more young
people, such as apprentices, journeymen, errand-boys, etc., than any other
seminary of vice in town" (*Lives*, p. 362).

[II.iii]   Macheath, *alone.*

MACHEATH.

What a fool is a fond wench. Polly is most confoundedly
bit. I love the sex. And a man who loves money might
as well be contented with one guinea as I with one woman.
The town perhaps hath been as much obliged to me for
recruiting it with freehearted ladies, as to any recruiting   5
officer in the army. If it were not for us and the other
gentlemen of the sword, Drury Lane would be uninhabited.

AIR XXI, *Would You Have a Young Virgin, etc.*   *very bawdy original*

If the heart of a man is depressed with cares,
The mist is dispelled when a woman appears;
Like the notes of a fiddle, she sweetly, sweetly   10
Raises the spirits, and charms our ears.
Roses and lilies her cheeks disclose,
But her ripe lips are more sweet than those.
   Press her,
   Caress her;   15
   With blisses,
   Her kisses
Dissolve us in pleasure, and soft repose.

I must have women. There is nothing unbends the mind like
them. Money is not so strong a cordial for the time. —Drawer!   20

Enter Drawer.

Is the porter gone for all the ladies, according to my
directions?

THE DRAWER.

I expect him back every minute. But you know, sir, you
sent him as far as Hockley in the Hole for three of the
ladies, for one in Vinegar Yard, and for the rest of them   25
somewhere about Lewkner's Lane. Sure some of them are

0.1. Macheath, *alone*] Macheath,
Drawer] *O1–2, Q*.

---

7. *Drury Lane*] the street synonymous with London prostitution.
25. *Vinegar Yard*] a small court south of the Theatre-Royal in Drury
Lane, opening into what was then Bridge, or Brydges, Street.
26. *Lewkner's Lane*] now Macklin Street. Jonathan Wild operated a
brothel there (Thornbury, III, 208).

below, for I hear the bar bell. As they come I will show
them up. —Coming, coming.   [*Exit.*]

[II.iv]
Macheath. [*To him enter*] Mrs. Coaxer, Dolly Trull, Mrs. Vixen,
Betty Doxy, Jenny Diver, Mrs. Slammekin, Suky Tawdry, *and*
Molly Brazen.

MACHEATH.

Dear Mrs. Coaxer, you are welcome. You look charmingly
today. I hope you don't want the repairs of quality, and
lay on paint. —Dolly Trull! Kiss me, you slut; are you
as amorous as ever, hussy? You are always so taken up with
stealing hearts that you don't allow yourself time to steal   5
anything else. —Ah Dolly, thou wilt ever be a coquette!
—Mrs. Vixen, I'm yours. I always loved a woman of wit
and spirit; they make charming mistresses, but plaguy
wives. —Betty Doxy! Come hither, hussy. Do you drink
as hard as ever? You had better stick to good, wholesome   10
beer; for in troth, Betty, strong waters will in time ruin
your constitution. You should leave those to your betters.
—What! And my pretty Jenny Diver too! As prim and
demure as ever! There is not any prude, though ever so high
bred, hath a more sanctified look with a more mischievous   15
heart. Ah! Thou art a dear, artful hypocrite. —Mrs.
Slammekin! As careless and genteel as ever! All you fine
ladies, who know your own beauty, affect an undress.
—But see, here's Suky Tawdry come to contradict what I
was saying. Everything she gets one way she lays out upon   20
her back. Why, Suky, you must keep at least a dozen tallymen. —Molly Brazen! (*She kisses him.*) That's well done.
I love a freehearted wench. Thou hast a most agreeable
assurance, girl, and art as willing as a turtle.

[*Harp music begins.*]

---

22. *tallymen*] "brokers that let out clothes to the women of the town"
(Grose). A *tally* was "a stick cut into two parts, on each whereof is marked,
with notches or otherwise, what is due between debtor and creditor. It was
the ancient mode of keeping accounts. One part was held by the creditor,
and the other by the debtor" (Black).
24. *turtle*] i.e., a turtle dove.

—But hark, I hear music. The harper is at the door. "If | 25
music be the food of love, play on." Ere you seat yourselves, •
ladies, what think you of a dance? Come in!

Enter harper.

Play the French tune that Mrs. Slammekin was so fond
of.

A dance à la ronde *in the French manner; near the end of it this song and
chorus.*

AIR XXII, *Cotillon*

MACHEATH.   Youth's the season made for joys;   30
                    Love is then our duty;
                    She alone who that employs
                    Well deserves her beauty.
                        Let's be gay
                        While we may;   35
                        Beauty's a flower despised in decay.
[CHORUS.]   Youth's the season, etc.

                    Let us drink and sport today;
                    Ours is not tomorrow.
                    Love with youth flies swift away;   40
                    Age is nought but sorrow.
                        Dance and sing;
                        Time's on the wing;
                        Life never knows the return of spring.
CHORUS.   Let us drink, etc.   45

MACHEATH.

Now, pray ladies, take your places. Here, fellow. *Pays the harper.*
Bid the drawer bring us more wine.   *Ex[it]* harper.
If any of the ladies choose gin, I hope they will be so free
to call for it.

JENNY DIVER.

You look as if you meant me. Wine is strong enough for 50
me. Indeed, sir, I never drink strong waters, but when I
have the colic.

MACHEATH.

Just the excuse of the fine ladies. Why, a lady of quality
is never without the colic. I hope, Mrs. Coaxer, you

have had good success of late in your visits among the   55
mercers.

MRS. COAXER.

We have so many interlopers. Yet with industry, one may
still have a little picking. I carried a silver-flowered lutestring and a piece of black paduasoy to Mr. Peachum's
lock but last week.   60

MRS. VIXEN.

There's Molly Brazen hath the ogle of a rattlesnake. She
riveted a linen draper's eye so fast upon her that he was
nicked of three pieces of cambric before he could look off.

MOLLY BRAZEN.

Oh dear madam! But sure nothing can come up to your
handling of laces! And then you have such a sweet deluding   65
tongue. To cheat a man is nothing; but the woman must
have fine parts indeed who cheats a woman!

MRS. VIXEN.

Lace, madam, lies in a small compass, and is of easy
conveyance. But you are apt, madam, to think too well of
your friends.   70

MRS. COAXER.

If any woman hath more art than another, to be sure, 'tis
Jenny Diver. Though her fellow be never so agreeable, she
can pick his pocket as coolly as if money were her only
pleasure. Now that is a command of the passions uncommon
in a woman!   75

JENNY DIVER.

I never go to the tavern with a man but in the view of
business. I have other hours, and other sort of men, for my
pleasure. But had I your address, madam—

MACHEATH.

Have done with your compliments, ladies, and drink about.
[*To* Jenny.]   You are not so fond of me, Jenny, as you   80
use to be.

JENNY DIVER.

'Tis not convenient, sir, to show my fondness among so

58–59. *lutestring . . . paduasoy*] expensive silks imported from France and
Holland (Gee, pp. 18, 19, 32, 34).

many rivals. 'Tis your own choice, and not the warmth of
my inclination, that will determine you.

AIR XXIII, *All in a Misty Morning, etc.*

Before the barndoor crowing,
   The cock by hens attended,   85
His eyes around him throwing,
   Stands for a while suspended.
Then one he singles from the crew,
   And cheers the happy hen,
With how do you do, and how do you do,   90
   And how do you do again.

MACHEATH.
   Ah Jenny, thou art a dear slut.
DOLLY TRULL.
   Pray, madam, were you ever in keeping?
SUKY TAWDRY.
   I hope, madam, I han't been so long upon the town, but I
have met with some good fortune as well as my neighbors. 95
DOLLY TRULL.
   Pardon me, madam, I meant no harm by the question; 'twas
only in the way of conversation.
SUKY TAWDRY.
   Indeed, madam, if I had not been a fool, I might have
lived very handsomely with my last friend. But upon his
missing five guineas, he turned me off. Now I never suspected 100
he had counted them.
MRS. SLAMMEKIN.
   Who do you look upon, madam, as your best sort of keepers?
DOLLY TRULL?
   That, madam, is thereafter as they be.
MRS. SLAMMEKIN.
   I, madam, was once kept by a Jew; and bating their
religion, to women they are a good sort of people.   105
SUKY TAWDRY.
   Now for my part, I own I like an old fellow, for we always
make them pay for what they can't do.

83.1. *etc.*] *O1–2; om. Q.*

MRS. VIXEN.

A spruce prentice, let me tell you, ladies, is no ill thing;
they bleed freely. I have sent at least two or three dozen
of them in my time to the plantations.   110

JENNY DIVER.

But to be sure, sir, with so much good fortune as you have
had upon the road, you must be grown immensely rich.

MACHEATH.

The road, indeed, hath done me justice, but the gaming-
table hath been my ruin.

AIR XXIV, *When Once I Lay with Another Man's Wife, etc.*

JENNY DIVER.

    The gamesters and lawyers are jugglers alike;   115
      If they meddle your all is in danger.
    Like gypsies, if once they can finger a souse,
    Your pockets they pick, and they pilfer your house,
      And give your estate to a stranger.

A man of courage should never put anything to the risk, 120
but his life.

[*She points to his pistols.*]

These are the tools of a man of honor.

She takes up his pistol.

Cards and dice are only fit for cowardly cheats, who prey
upon their friends.

SUKY TAWDRY.

(Tawdry *takes up the other* [*pistol*].)
This, sir, is fitter for your hand. Besides your loss of money, 125
'tis a loss to the ladies. Gaming takes you off from women.
How fond could I be of you! But before company, 'tis ill
bred.

108–110. *A spruce ... plantations*] i.e., two or three dozen apprentices
became thieves to support Mrs. Vixen, and when caught they were transported (cf. I.ii.27).
  115. *jugglers*] magicians, masters of sleight of hand.
  117. *souse*] a *sou*, a small amount of money.

MACHEATH.

Wanton hussies!

JENNY DIVER.

I must and will have a kiss to give my wine a zest. 130

They take him about the neck, and make signs to Peachum and constables, who rush in upon him.

[II.v] *To them, Peachum and constables.*

PEACHUM.

I seize you, sir, as my prisoner.

MACHEATH.

Was this well done, Jenny? —Women are decoy ducks; who can trust them! Beasts, jades, jilts, harpies, furies, whores!

PEACHUM.

Your case, Mr. Macheath, is not particular. The greatest 5 heroes have been ruined by women. But, to do them justice, I must own they are a pretty sort of creatures, if we could trust them. You must now, sir, take your leave of the ladies, and if they have a mind to make you a visit, they will be sure to find you at home. The gentleman, ladies, 10 lodges in Newgate. Constables, wait upon the Captain to his lodgings.

AIR XXV, *When First I Laid Siege to My Chloris, etc.*

MACHEATH. At the tree I shall suffer with pleasure,
    At the tree I shall suffer with pleasure;
     Let me go where I will, 15
     In all kinds of ill,
    I shall find no such furies as these are.

12.1. *etc.*] *O1–2; om. Q.*

130.1–2. *They . . . him*] Criminals were often apprehended in this way. For example, Kate Leonard persuaded Edward Burnworth to stay in her room for a meal, and then she informed six men, who arrested Burnworth (*A True and Exact Account of the Lives of Edward Burnworth Alias Frazier, William Blewitt, Thomas Berry, and Emanuel Dickenson* [London: John Applebee, 1726], p. 19). Hogarth pictured such a scene in Plate IX of *Industry and Idleness.*

PEACHUM.

　　Ladies, I'll take care the reckoning shall be discharged.

　　　　　　Ex[it] Macheath, *guarded, with* Peachum *and constables.*

[II.vi]　　　　　　　　*The women remain.*

MRS. VIXEN.

　　Look ye, Mrs. Jenny, though Mr. Peachum may have made
　　a private bargain with you and Suky Tawdry for betraying
　　the Captain, as we were all assisting, we ought all to share
　　alike.

MRS. COAXER.

　　I think Mr. Peachum, after so long an acquaintance, might　　5
　　have trusted me as well as Jenny Diver.

MRS. SLAMMEKIN.

　　I am sure at least three men of his hanging, and in a year's
　　time too (if he did me justice), should be set down to my
　　account.

DOLLY TRULL.

　　Mrs. Slammekin, that is not fair. For you know one of　　10
　　them was taken in bed with me.

JENNY DIVER.

　　As far as a bowl of punch or a treat, I believe Mrs. Suky
　　will join with me. As for anything else, ladies, you cannot
　　in conscience expect it.

MRS. SLAMMEKIN.

　　Dear madam—　　　　　　The ladies go out　　15

DOLLY TRULL.

　　I would not for the world—　　politely deferring to

MRS. SLAMMEKIN.　　　　　　　one another – curtseying

　　'Tis impossible for me—　　　　(parody v ladies

DOLLY TRULL.　　　　　　　　　　　　　of fashion)

　　As I hope to be saved, madam—

MRS. SLAMMEKIN.

　　Nay, then I must stay here all night—

DOLLY TRULL.

　　Since you command me.　　　　*Exeunt with great ceremony.*　　20

[II.vii]　　　　　　　*Newgate.*

[*Enter*] Lockit, *turnkeys*, Macheath, *constables.*

LOCKIT.

Noble Captain, you are welcome. You have not been a
lodger of mine this year and half. You know the custom,
sir. Garnish, Captain, garnish. Hand me down those
fetters there.

MACHEATH.

Those, Mr. Lockit, seem to be the heaviest of the whole　5
set. With your leave, I should like the further pair better.

LOCKIT.

Look ye, Captain, we know what is fittest for our prisoners.
When a gentleman uses me with civility, I always do
the best I can to please him. —Hand them down I say.
—We have them of all prices, from one guinea to ten,　10
and 'tis fitting every gentleman should please himself.

MACHEATH.

I understand you, sir. (*Gives money.*)　The fees here are
so many, and so exorbitant, that few fortunes can bear the
expense of getting off handsomely, or of dying like a
gentleman.　　　　　　　　　　　　　　　　　　　　15

LOCKIT.

Those, I see, will fit the Captain better. —Take down the
further pair. Do but examine them, sir. Never was better

---

1. S.P. LOCKIT] At the time of *The Beggar's Opera*, English prisons were
managed by private persons and corporations who paid a large security
to the Crown for the privilege of exclusive concession. All persons employed
in a jail—the principal jailer like Lockit, turnkeys, guards, mess men,
errand boys, and others—were low salaried or unsalaried, and some even
paid their superiors for their jobs. These men were legally entitled to exact
fees from their prisoners (see Hogarth's *Rake's Progress*, Plate VII), who were
thus forced to pay exorbitant charges for light chains (heavy chains were
apparently free), food, bedding, liquor, candles, housecleaning, walking
space, and all other necessities and comforts. There was no way out of this
financial trap; even prisoners acquitted of crimes could not get out of jail
unless their jail fees were paid. Thus, Lockit's charges for chains, though
outrageous, are legal.

3. *garnish*] that custom in English prisons whereby each prisoner entering
for the first time was compelled to buy drinks for the other prisoners. If the
new prisoner had no money, the other prisoners stripped him and sold his
clothes to pay for the liquor (probably sold at inflated cost by the jailer).
Cf. Fielding's *Amelia*, I.iii, and the modern words *garnishee, garnishment.*

sales pitch

work. How genteelly they are made! They will fit as easy as a glove, and the nicest man in England might not be ashamed to wear them. (*He puts on the chains.*) If I had 20 the best gentleman in the land in my custody, I could not equip him more handsomely. And so, sir, I now leave you to your private meditations.

[*Exeunt* Lockit, *turnkeys, constables.*]

[II.viii] Macheath [*alone*].

AIR XXVI, *Courtiers, Courtiers, Think It No Harm, etc.*

MACHEATH. Man may escape from rope and gun;
    Nay, some have outlived the doctor's pill;
Who takes a woman must be undone;
    That basilisk is sure to kill.
The fly that sips treacle is lost in the sweets, 5
So he that tastes woman, woman, woman,
    He that tastes woman, ruin meets.

To what a woeful plight have I brought myself. Here must I (all day long, till I am hanged) be confined to hear the reproaches of a wench who lays her ruin at my door. I am 10 in the custody of her father, and to be sure if he knows of the matter, I shall have a fine time on't betwixt this and my execution. But I promised the wench marriage. What signifies a promise to a woman? Does not man in marriage itself promise a hundred things that he never 15 means to perform? Do all we can, women will believe us, for they look upon a promise as an excuse for following their own inclinations. —But here comes Lucy, and I cannot get from her. Would I were deaf!

marriage
(promises to women)

[II.ix] Macheath. [*To him enter*] Lucy.

LUCY. You base man you! How can you look me in the face after what hath passed between us? See here, perfidious wretch, how I am forced to bear about the load of infamy you have

[II.viii]
0.2. *etc.*] *O1–2; om.* Q.

---

4. *basilisk*] a mythical reptile with a lethal breath and stare.

laid upon me. Oh Macheath, thou hast robbed me of my
quiet. To see thee tortured would give me pleasure!   5

AIR XXVII, *A Lovely Lass to a Friar Came, etc.*

Thus when a good huswife sees a rat
In her trap in the morning taken,
With pleasure her heart goes pitapat,
In revenge for her loss of bacon.
Then she throws him   10
To the dog or cat,
To be worried, crushed, and shaken.

MACHEATH.
Have you no bowels, no tenderness, my dear Lucy, to see a
husband in these circumstances?

LUCY.
A husband?   15

MACHEATH.
In every respect but the form, and that, my dear, may be
said over us at any time. Friends should not insist upon
ceremonies. From a man of honor, his word is as good as
his bond.

LUCY.
'Tis the pleasure of all you fine men to insult the women   20
you have ruined.

AIR XXVIII, *'Twas When the Sea Was Roaring, etc.*

How cruel are the traitors
Who lie and swear in jest,
To cheat unguarded creatures
Of virtue, fame, and rest!   25
Whoever steals a shilling,
Through shame the guilt conceals;
In love the perjured villain
With boasts the theft reveals.

5.1. *etc.*] *O1–2; om. Q.*   21.1. *etc.*] *O1–2; om. Q.*

5. *tortured*] In Newgate there was a "press yard," where heavy weights
were laid upon recalcitrant prisoners who, in order to prevent their possessions from being turned over to their captors, refused to enter a plea of
guilty or not guilty. This was the only legal torture (*peine forte et dure*), and
it was kept up until the prisoners either entered a plea or died.

MACHEATH.

The very first opportunity, my dear (have but patience),   30
you shall be my wife in whatever manner you please.

LUCY.

Insinuating monster! And so you think I know nothing of the
affair of Miss Polly Peachum. I could tear thy eyes out!

MACHEATH.

Sure, Lucy, you can't be such a fool as to be jealous of
Polly!   35

LUCY.

Are you not married to her, you brute, you?

MACHEATH.

Married! Very good. The wench gives it out only to vex
thee, and to ruin me in thy good opinion. 'Tis true, I go
to the house. I chat with the girl, I kiss her, I say a thousand
things to her (as all gentlemen do) that mean nothing,   40
to divert myself. And now the silly jade hath set it about
that I am married to her, to let me know what she would
be at. Indeed, my dear Lucy, these violent passions
may be of ill consequence to a woman in your condition.

LUCY.

Come, come, Captain, for all your assurance, you know that   45
Miss Polly hath put it out of your power to do me the justice
you promised me.

MACHEATH.

A jealous woman believes everything her passion suggests.
To convince you of my sincerity, if we can find the Ordinary,
I shall have no scruples of making you my wife; and I   50
know the consequence of having two at a time.

LUCY.

That you are only to be hanged, and so get rid of them both.

MACHEATH.

I am ready, my dear Lucy, to give you satisfaction, if you
think there is any in marriage. What can a man of honor
say more?   55

LUCY.

So then it seems you are not married to Miss Polly.

---

49. *Ordinary*] As an ordained priest, the Ordinary could perform
weddings.

MACHEATH.

You know, Lucy, the girl is prodigiously conceited. No
man can say a civil thing to her, but (like other fine ladies)
her vanity makes her think he's her own forever and
ever.   60

AIR XXIX, *The Sun Had Loosed His Weary Teams, etc.*

The first time at the looking glass
    The mother sets her daughter,
The image strikes the smiling lass
    With self-love ever after.
Each time she looks, she, fonder grown,   65
    Thinks ev'ry charm grows stronger;
But alas, vain maid, all eyes but your own
    Can see you are not younger.

When women consider their own beauties, they are all alike
unreasonable in their demands; for they expect their lovers   70
should like them as long as they like themselves.

LUCY.

Yonder is my father. Perhaps this way we may light upon
the Ordinary, who shall try if you will be as good as your
word. For I long to be made an honest woman.

[*Exit* Lucy. *The curtain closes on* Macheath, *leaving the stage clear for the
next scene.*]

[II.x]   [*Scene, another part of the prison.*]
            [*Enter*] Peachum [*and*] Lockit *with an account book.*

LOCKIT.

In this last affair, Brother Peachum, we are agreed. You
have consented to go halves in Macheath.

PEACHUM.

We shall never fall out about an execution. But as to that
article, pray how stands our last year's account?

LOCKIT.

If you will run your eye over it, you'll find 'tis fair and   5
clearly stated.

60.1. *etc.*] *O1–2; om. Q.*

PEACHUM. *Acheta*

    This long arrear of the government is very hard upon us!
Can it be expected that we should hang our acquaintance
for nothing, when our betters will hardly save theirs without
being paid for it? Unless the people in employment pay   10
better, I promise them for the future, I shall let other
rogues live besides their own.

LOCKIT.

    Perhaps, brother, they are afraid these matters may be
carried too far. We are treated too by them with contempt,
as if our profession were not reputable.   15

PEACHUM.

    In one respect indeed, our employment may be reckoned
dishonest, because, like great statesmen, we encourage
those who betray their friends.

LOCKIT.

    Such language, brother, anywhere else, might turn to your
prejudice. Learn to be more guarded, I beg you.   20

            AIR XXX, *How Happy Are We, etc.*

      When you censure the age,
        Be cautious and sage,
    Lest the courtiers offended should be;
      If you mention vice or bribe,
      'Tis so pat to all the tribe,   25
    Each cries, "That was leveled at me."

PEACHUM.

    Here's poor Ned Clincher's name, I see. Sure, Brother
Lockit, there was a little unfair proceeding in Ned's case; for

---

    7. *This . . . us*] In considering the difficulty of collecting rewards under
the Highwayman Act, Fielding said in 1751: "Sometimes even when the
felon is properly convicted, I have been told that the money does not come
so easily and fully to the pockets of those who are entitled to it as it ought"
(Fielding, p. 106).

    27. *Ned Clincher's name*] from *to clinch*, "to confirm an improbable story by
another" (Grose). Hence, a clincher was a perjurer. Cf. Swift's poem
"Clever Tom Clinch going to be hanged," in *The Poems of Jonathan Swift*, ed.
Harold Williams [Oxford, 1937], II, 399 f.

    28. *Ned's case*] Though Lockit's previous activities have been legal, here
Gay suggests a way in which prison keepers were corrupt. Ned Clincher
has apparently paid Lockit for delaying his execution, and Lockit by

he told me in the condemned hold that for value received
you had promised him a session or two longer without   30
molestation.

LOCKIT.

Mr. Peachum, this is the first time my honor was ever called
in question.

PEACHUM.

Business is at an end, if once we act dishonorably.

LOCKIT.

Who accuses me?   35

PEACHUM.

You are warm, brother.

LOCKIT.

He that attacks my honor attacks my livelihood. And this
usage, sir, is not to be borne.

PEACHUM.

Since you provoke me to speak, I must tell you too that Mrs.
Coaxer charges you with defrauding her of her information 40
money for the apprehending of Curl-Pated Hugh. Indeed,
indeed, brother, we must punctually pay our spies, or we
shall have no information.

LOCKIT.

Is this language to me, sirrah, who have saved you from the
gallows, sirrah!   45

Collaring each other.

PEACHUM.

If I am hanged, it shall be for ridding the world of an
arrant rascal.

---

accepting the money has committed an illegal act. Peachum does not
object to the bribe, but to the fact that Lockit has betrayed Ned by sending
him to the gallows anyway.

35-36. *Who . . . brother*] The argument between Peachum and Lockit
alludes to the worsening relations between Walpole and his brother-in-law,
Townshend. Shortly after the first performances of *The Beggar's Opera*,
Walpole and Townshend actually did collar each other, and Gay's scene
thus gained in topicality. See Jean B. Kern, "A Note on *The Beggar's
Opera*," *Philological Quarterly*, XVII (1938), 411–413. The quarrel is
described in Schultz, p. 187.

42. *our spies*] perhaps an allusion to the secret methods by which Walpole
gained evidence against Bishop Atterbury in 1722.

Self-interest

LOCKIT.

This hand shall do the office of the halter you deserve, and throttle you—you dog!

PEACHUM.

Brother, brother, we are both in the wrong. We shall be both   50
losers in the dispute, for you know we have it in our power
to hang each other. You should not be so passionate.

LOCKIT.

Nor you so provoking.

PEACHUM.

'Tis our mutual interest; 'tis for the interest of the world
we should agree. If I said anything, brother, to the prejudice   55
of your character, I ask pardon.

LOCKIT.

Brother Peachum, I can forgive as well as resent. Give me
your hand. Suspicion does not become a friend.

PEACHUM.

I only meant to give you occasion to justify yourself. But
I must now step home, for I expect the gentleman about   60
this snuffbox, that Filch nimmed two nights ago in the park.
I appointed him at this hour.   [*Exit.*]

[II.xi]   Lockit. [*To him enter*] Lucy.

LOCKIT.

Whence come you, hussy?

LUCY.

My tears might answer that question.

LOCKIT.

You have then been whimpering and fondling, like a spaniel,
over the fellow that hath abused you.

LUCY.

One can't help love; one can't cure it. 'Tis not in my   5
power to obey you, and hate him.

LOCKIT.

Learn to bear your husband's death like a reasonable
woman. 'Tis not the fashion, nowadays, so much as to
affect sorrow upon these occasions. No woman would ever
marry if she had not the chance of mortality for a release.   10
Act like a woman of spirit, hussy, and thank your father
for what he is doing.

AIR XXXI, *Of a Noble Race Was Shenkin*

LUCY.
Is then his fate decreed, sir?
Such a man can I think of quitting?
When first we met, so moves me yet,   15
Oh, see how my heart is splitting!

LOCKIT.
Look ye, Lucy, there is no saving him. So, I think, you
must ev'n do like other widows: buy yourself weeds and be
cheerful.   *mourning*

AIR XXXII

You'll think, e'er many days ensue,   20
This sentence not severe;
I hang your husband, child, 'tis true,
But with him hang your care.
Twang dang dillo dee.

Like a good wife, go moan over your dying husband. That,   25
child, is your duty. Consider, girl, you can't have the man
and the money too. So make yourself as easy as you can by
getting all you can from him.   [*Exeunt.*]

[II.xii]   [*Scene, Macheath's cell.*]
Macheath. [*To him enter*] Lucy.

LUCY.
Though the Ordinary was out of the way today, I hope, my
dear, you will, upon the first opportunity, quiet my scruples
—Oh sir! My father's hard heart is not to be softened, and
I am in the utmost despair.

MACHEATH.
But if I could raise a small sum— Would not twenty   5
guineas, think you, move him? Of all the arguments in
the way of business, the perquisite is the most prevailing.
Your father's perquisites for the escape of prisoners must
amount to a considerable sum in the year. Money well
timed, and properly applied, will do anything.   10

Money

13. S.P. LUCY] *O1–2*; Polly *Q.*

AIR XXXIII, *London Ladies*

If you at an office solicit your due,
  And would not have matters neglected,
You must quicken the clerk with the perquisite too
  To do what his duty directed.
Or would you the frowns of a lady prevent,   15
  She too has this palpable failing;
The perquisite softens her into consent;
  That reason with all is prevailing.

LUCY.

What love or money can do shall be done, for all my
comfort depends upon your safety.   20

[II.xiii]   Lucy, Macheath. [*To them enter*] Polly.

POLLY.

Where is my dear husband? Was a rope ever intended for
this neck? Oh, let me throw my arms about it, and throttle
thee with love!   [Macheath *turns his back to her.*]   Why dost
thou turn away from me? 'Tis thy Polly! 'Tis thy wife!

MACHEATH.

Was ever such an unfortunate rascal as I am?   5

LUCY.

Was there ever such another villain?

POLLY.

Oh Macheath, was it for this we parted? Taken! Im-
prisoned! Tried! Hanged! Cruel reflection! I'll stay with
thee till death. No force shall tear thy dear wife from thee
now. —What means my love? Not one kind word? Not one   10
kind look? Think what thy Polly suffers to see thee in this
condition.

AIR XXXIV, *All in the Downs, etc.*

Thus when the swallow, seeking prey,
  Within the sash is closely pent,
His consort with bemoaning lay,   15
  Without sits pining for th'event.
Her chattering lovers all around her skim;
She heeds them not (poor bird); her soul's with him.

MACHEATH (*aside*).

    I must disown her. [*To* Lucy.]   The wench is distracted.

LUCY.

    Am I then bilked of my virtue? Can I have no reparation?   20
Sure men were born to lie, and women to believe them! Oh
villain! Villain!

POLLY.

    Am I not thy wife? Thy neglect of me, thy aversion to
me, too severely proves it. Look on me. Tell me, am I
not thy wife?   25

LUCY.

    Perfidious wretch!

POLLY.

    Barbarous husband!

LUCY.

    Hadst thou been hanged five months ago, I had been happy.

POLLY.

    And I too. If you had been kind to me till death, it would
not have vexed me. And that's no very unreasonable   30
request (though from a wife) to a man who hath not above
seven or eight days to live.

LUCY.

    Art thou then married to another? Has thou two wives,
monster?

MACHEATH.

    If women's tongues can cease for an answer, hear me.   35

LUCY.

    I won't. Flesh and blood can't bear my usage.

POLLY.

    Shall I not claim my own? Justice bids me speak.

    AIR XXXV, *Have You Heard of a Frolicsome Ditty, etc.*

MACHEATH.   How happy could I be with either,
           Were t'other dear charmer away.
      But while you thus tease me together,   40
           To neither a word will I say,
           But tol de rol, etc.

19. S.D. *To* Lucy] *NC.*   37.1. *etc.*] *O1–2; om. Q.*

POLLY.

Sure, my dear, there ought to be some preference shown
to a wife. At least she may claim the appearance of it.
[*Aside.*] He must be distracted with his misfortunes, or   45
he could not use me thus.

LUCY.

Oh villain, villain! Thou hast deceived me. I could even
inform against thee with pleasure. Not a prude wishes more
heartily to have facts against her intimate acquaintance,
than I now wish to have facts against thee. I would have   50
her satisfaction, and they should all out.

AIR XXXVI, *Irish Trot*

POLLY.   I'm bubbled.
LUCY.   I'm bubbled.
POLLY.   Oh how I am troubled!
LUCY.   Bamboozled, and bit!
POLLY.   My distresses are doubled.
LUCY.   When you come to the tree, should the hangman refuse,   55
          These fingers, with pleasure, could fasten the noose.
POLLY.   I'm bubbled, etc.

MACHEATH.

Be pacified, my dear Lucy. This is all a fetch of Polly's
to make me desperate with you in case I get off. If I am
hanged, she would fain have the credit of being thought my   60
widow. [*To* Polly.] Really, Polly, this is no time for a
dispute of this sort; for whenever you are talking of marriage,
I am thinking of hanging.

POLLY.

And hast thou the heart to persist in disowning me?

MACHEATH.

And hast thou the heart to persist in persuading me that   65
I am married? Why, Polly, dost thou seek to aggravate my
misfortunes?

LUCY.

Really, Miss Peachum, you but expose yourself. Besides,

---

58. *fetch*] deceit, ruse.

'tis barbarous in you to worry a gentleman in his circumstances.   70

AIR XXXVII

POLLY.   Cease your funning;
                    Force or cunning
                Never shall my heart trepan. *deceive*
                    All these sallies
                    Are but malice   75
                To seduce my constant man.
                    'Tis most certain,
                    By their flirting
                Women oft have envy shown:
                    Pleased, to ruin   80
                    Others wooing,
                Never happy in their own!

Decency, madam, methinks might teach you to behave
yourself with some reserve with the husband, while his
wife is present.   85

MACHEATH.
But seriously, Polly, this is carrying the joke a little too
far.

LUCY.
If you are determined, madam, to raise a disturbance in the
prison, I shall be obliged to send for the turnkey to show
you the door. I am sorry, madam, you force me to be so   90
ill-bred.

POLLY.
Give me leave to tell you, madam, these forward airs don't
become you in the least, madam. And my duty, madam,
obliges me to stay with my husband, madam.

AIR XXXVIII, *Good Morrow, Gossip Joan*

LUCY.   Why how now, Madam Flirt?   95
                    If you thus must chatter,
                And are for flinging dirt,
                    Let's try who best can spatter,
                    Madam Flirt!

POLLY. Why how now, saucy jade?   100
   Sure the wench is tipsy!
   (*To him.*) How can you see me made
   The scoff of such a gypsy?
   (*To her.*) Saucy jade!

[II.xiv] Lucy, Macheath, Polly. [*Enter to them*] Peachum.

PEACHUM.

 Where's my wench? Ah hussy, hussy! Come you home, you
 slut; and when your fellow is hanged, hang yourself, to
 make your family some amends.

POLLY [*to* Peachum].

 Dear, dear father, do not tear me from him. I must speak;
 I have more to say to him. [*To* Macheath.] Oh, twist thy 5
 fetters about me, that he may not haul me from thee.

PEACHUM.

 Sure all women are alike. If ever they commit the folly,
 they are sure to commit another by exposing themselves.
 Away! Not a word more. You are my prisoner now, hussy.

AIR XXXIX, *Irish Howl*

POLLY. No power on earth can e'er divide   10
   The knot that sacred love hath tied.
   When parents draw against our mind,
   The truelove's knot they faster bind.
    Oh, oh ray, oh Amborah—oh, oh, etc.

[*Exeunt* Peachum *and* Polly, *she*] *holding* Macheath, Peachum *pulling
her* [*offstage*].

[II.xv]   Lucy, Macheath.

MACHEATH.

 I am naturally compassionate, wife, so that I could not use

[II.xiv]   in ambora = ho an *Q* (*in* "*Songs
14. Oh, . . . oh] *O1–2, Q*; Ho ho ra in* '*The Beggar's Opera*'").

the wench as she deserved; which made you at first suspect
there was something in what she said.

LUCY.

Indeed, my dear, I was strangely puzzled.

MACHEATH.

If that had been the case, her father would never have   5
brought me into this circumstance. No, Lucy, I had rather
die than be false to thee.

LUCY.

How happy am I, if you say this from your heart! For I
love thee so, that I could sooner bear to see thee hanged
than in the arms of another.   10

MACHEATH.

But couldst thou bear to see me hanged?

LUCY.

Oh Macheath, I can never live to see that day.

MACHEATH.

You see, Lucy, in the account of love you are in my debt,
and you must now be convinced that I rather choose to die
than be another's. Make me, if possible, love thee more,   15
and let me owe my life to thee. If you refuse to assist me,
Peachum and your father will immediately put me beyond
all means of escape.

LUCY.

My father, I know, hath been drinking hard with the
prisoners, and I fancy he is now taking his nap in his own   20
room. If I can procure the keys, shall I go off with thee,
my dear?

MACHEATH.

If we are together, 'twill be impossible to lie concealed.
As soon as the search begins to be a little cool, I will send
to thee. Till then my heart is thy prisoner.   25

LUCY.

Come then, my dear husband, owe thy life to me, and
though you love me not, be grateful. But that Polly runs in
my head strangely.

MACHEATH.

A moment of time may make us unhappy forever.

–57–

AIR XL, *The Lass of Patie's Mill, etc.*

LUCY.

I like the fox shall grieve,   30
    Whose mate hath left her side,
Whom hounds, from morn to eve,
    Chase o'er the country wide.
Where can my lover hide?
    Where cheat the wary pack?   35
If love be not his guide,
    He never will come back.   [*Exeunt.*]

[*End of the Second Act.*]

29.1. *etc.*] *O1–2; om. Q.*   35. wary] *O2* (*some copies*), *Q*; weary *O1, O2* (*some copies*).

ACT III

[III.i]   *Scene, Newgate.*

[*Enter*] Lockit, Lucy.

LOCKIT.

To be sure, wench, you must have been aiding and abetting
to help him to this escape.

LUCY.

Sir, here hath been Peachum and his daughter Polly, and to
be sure they know the ways of Newgate as well as if they
had been born and bred in the place all their lives. Why   5
must all your suspicion light upon me?

LOCKIT.

Lucy, Lucy, I will have none of these shuffling answers.

LUCY.

Well then. If I know anything of him I wish I may be
burnt!

LOCKIT.

Keep your temper, Lucy, or I shall pronounce you guilty.   10

LUCY.

Keep yours, sir. I do wish I may be burnt. I do. And
what can I say more to convince you?

LOCKIT.

Did he tip handsomely? How much did he come down with?
Come hussy, don't cheat your father, and I shall not be
angry with you. Perhaps you have made a better bargain   15
with him than I could have done. How much, my good girl?

LUCY.

You know, sir, I am fond of him, and would have given
money to have kept him with me.

LOCKIT.

Ah Lucy! Thy education might have put thee more upon

8–9. *I wish . . . burnt*] All first offenders receiving benefit of clergy were
branded in the right thumb with an iron, shaped as a *T* for "thief." The
iron was either red hot or cold, depending upon the offense and also,
according to some claims, upon the amount of money the offender could
give the executioner, who administered the branding. Once a thief was
branded, he would receive the death sentence the next time he was convicted
of a felony.

thy guard, for a girl in the bar of an alehouse is always   20
besieged.

LUCY.

Dear sir, mention not my education, for 'twas to that I
owe my ruin.

AIR XLI, *If Love's a Sweet Passion, etc.*

When young at the bar you first taught me to score,
And bid me be free of my lips, and no more,   25
I was kissed by the parson, the squire, and the sot;
When the guest was departed, the kiss was forgot.
But his kiss was so sweet, and so closely he pressed,
That I languished and pined till I granted the rest.

If you can forgive me, sir, I will make a fair confession, for   30
to be sure he hath been a most barbarous villain to me.

LOCKIT.

And so you have let him escape, hussy. Have you?

LUCY.

When a woman loves, a kind look, a tender word, can persuade her to anything. And I could ask no other bribe.

LOCKIT.

Thou wilt always be a vulgar slut, Lucy. If you would not be   35
looked upon as a fool, you should never do anything but
upon the foot of interest. Those that act otherwise are
their own bubbles.

LUCY.

But love, sir, is a misfortune that may happen to the most
discreet woman, and in love we are all fools alike. Not-   40
withstanding all he swore, I am now fully convinced
that Polly Peachum is actually his wife. Did I let him
escape (fool that I was!) to go to her? Polly will wheedle
herself into his money, and then Peachum will hang him,
and cheat us both.   45

LOCKIT.

So I am to be ruined because, forsooth, you must be in
love! A very pretty excuse!

LUCY.

I could murder that impudent happy strumpet. I gave
him his life, and that creature enjoys the sweets of it.
Ungrateful Macheath!   50

AIR XLII, *South Sea Ballad*

My love is all madness and folly,
   Alone I lie,
   Toss, tumble, and cry,
What a happy creature is Polly!
Was e'er such a wretch as I!   55
With rage I redden like scarlet,
That my dear inconstant varlet,
   Stark blind to my charms,
   Is lost in the arms
Of that jilt, that inveigling harlot!   60
   Stark blind to my charms
   Is lost in the arms
Of that jilt, that inveigling harlot!
This, this my resentment alarms.

LOCKIT.

And so, after all this mischief, I must stay here to be   65
entertained with your caterwauling, Mistress Puss! Out
of my sight, wanton strumpet! You shall fast and mortify
yourself into reason, with now and then a little handsome
discipline to bring you to your senses. Go.   [*Exit* Lucy.]

[III.ii]   Lockit [*alone*].

LOCKIT.

Peachum then intends to outwit me in this affair, but I'll
be even with him. The dog is leaky in his liquor, so I'll
ply him that way, get the secret from him, and turn this
affair to my own advantage. Lions, wolves, and vultures
don't live together in herds, droves, or flocks. Of all animals   5
of prey, man is the only sociable one. Every one of us
preys upon his neighbor, and yet we herd together. Peachum
is my companion, my friend. According to the custom of
the world, indeed, he may quote thousands of precedents
for cheating me. And shall I not make use of the privilege   10
of friendship to make him a return?

AIR XLIII, *Packington's Pound*

Thus gamesters united in friendship are found,
Though they know that their industry all is a cheat;

-61-

They flock to their prey at the dicebox's sound,
And join to promote one another's deceit.   15
  But if by mishap
  They fail of a chap,
To keep in their hands, they each other entrap.
Like pikes, lank with hunger, who miss of their ends,
They bite their companions, and prey on their friends.   20

Now, Peachum, you and I, like honest tradesmen, are to
have a fair trial which of us two can overreach the other.
—Lucy!

Enter Lucy.

Are there any of Peachum's people now in the house?

LUCY.

Filch, sir, is drinking a quartern of strong waters in the   25
next room with Black Moll.

LOCKIT.

Bid him come to me.   [*Exit* Lucy.]

[III.iii]   Lockit. [*Enter to him*] Filch.

LOCKIT.

Why, boy, thou lookest as if thou wert half starved, like a
shotten herring.

FILCH.

One had need have the constitution of a horse to go through
the business. Since the favorite child-getter was disabled
by a mishap, I have picked up a little money by helping   5
the ladies to a pregnancy against their being called down
to sentence. But if a man cannot get an honest livelihood
any easier way, I am sure 'tis what I can't undertake
for another session.

LOCKIT.

Truly, if that great man should tip off, 'twould be an   10

---

19. *pikes*] Pikes are known for their voraciousness.
[III.iii]
  2. *shotten*] depleted of spawn.
  5–7. *I . . . sentence*] cf. note to I.ii.4. Misson states that, though women
"came never so good Virgins into the Prison, there are a set of Wags there
that take Care of those Matters" (*M. Misson's Memoirs and Observations
in His Travels over England*, tr. John Ozell [London, 1719], pp. 329 f.).

irreparable loss. The vigor and prowess of a knight-errant
never saved half the ladies in distress that he hath done.
But, boy, canst thou tell me where thy master is to be
found?

FILCH.

At his lock, sir, at the Crooked Billet.   15

LOCKIT.

Very well. I have nothing more with you.   (*Ex[it]* Filch.)
I'll go to him there, for I have many important affairs to
settle with him. And in the way of those transactions, I'll
artfully get into his secret. So that Macheath shall not
remain a day longer out of my clutches.   [*Exit.*]   20

[III.iv]   *Scene, a gaming-house.*
[*Enter*] Macheath *in a fine tarnished coat*, Ben Budge, Matt of the Mint.

MACHEATH.

I am sorry, gentlemen, the road was so barren of money.
When my friends are in difficulties, I am always glad that
my fortune can be serviceable to them.   (*Gives them money.*)
You see, gentlemen, I am not a mere court friend, who
professes everything and will do nothing.   5

AIR XLIV, *Lillibulero*

The modes of the court so common are grown,
    That a true friend can hardly be met;
Friendship for interest is but a loan,
    Which they let out for what they can get.
        'Tis true, you find   10
        Some friends so kind,
Who will give you good counsel themselves to defend.
        In sorrowful ditty
        They promise, they pity,
But shift you for money, from friend to friend.   15

But we, gentlemen, have still honor enough to break through
the corruptions of the world. And while I can serve you,
you may command me.

BEN BUDGE.

It grieves my heart that so generous a man should be
involved in such difficulties as oblige him to live with   20
such ill company, and herd with gamesters.

MATT OF THE MINT.

See the partiality of mankind. One man may steal a horse, better than another look over a hedge. Of all mechanics, of all servile handicraftsmen, a gamester is the vilest. But yet, as many of the quality are of the profession, he is admitted amongst the politest company. I wonder we are not more respected.   25

MACHEATH.

There will be deep play tonight at Marybone, and consequently money may be picked up upon the road. Meet me there, and I'll give you the hint who is worth setting.   30

MATT OF THE MINT.

The fellow with a brown coat with a narrow gold binding, I am told, is never without money.

MACHEATH.

What do you mean, Matt? Sure you will not think of meddling with him! He's a good honest kind of a fellow, and one of us.   35

BEN BUDGE.

To be sure, sir, we will put ourselves under your direction.

MACHEATH.

Have an eye upon the moneylenders. A rouleau, or two, would prove a pretty sort of an expedition. I hate extortion.

MATT OF THE MINT.

Those rouleaus are very pretty things. I hate your bank bills; there is such a hazard in putting them off.   40

22–23. *One . . . hedge*] cf. Air LXVII. The idea is that a man of quality or influence may steal with impunity, while a man of no influence cannot get away with even the slightest wrong.

23. *mechanics*] manual workers.

30. *setting*] robbing, setting upon to rob.

37. *moneylenders*] Moneylenders hovered around the gambling dens to lend money at usurious rates. For the portrait of a moneylender in action, see Plate VI of Hogarth's *Rake's Progress*.

37. *rouleau*] "a number of guineas, from twenty to fifty or more, wrapped up in paper, for the more ready circulation at gaming-tables: sometimes they are inclosed in ivory boxes, made to hold exactly 20, 50, or 100 guineas" (Grose).

38. *extortion*] robbing a person by putting him "in fear," a hanging offense even for first offenders.

39–40. *bank bills*] See note to I.iv.39–40.

MACHEATH.

There is a certain man of distinction who in his time hath
nicked me out of a great deal of the ready. He is in my
cash, Ben. I'll point him out to you this evening, and you
shall draw upon him for the debt. The company are met; I
hear the dicebox in the other room. So, gentlemen, your   45
servant. You'll meet me at Marybone.   [*Exeunt.*]

[III.v]   *Scene, Peachum's lock.*
               A table with wine, brandy, pipes, and tobacco.
               [*Enter*] Peachum, Lockit, [*and servant*].

LOCKIT.

The Coronation account, Brother Peachum, is of so
intricate a nature that I believe it will never be settled.

PEACHUM.

It consists indeed of a great variety of articles. It was
worth to our people, in fees of different kinds, above ten
installments. This is part of the account, brother, that lies   5
open before us.

LOCKIT [*reading*].

"A lady's tail of rich brocade"—that, I see, is disposed of.

PEACHUM.

To Mrs. Diana Trapes, the tallywoman, and she will
make a good hand on't in shoes and slippers, to trick out
young ladies upon their going into keeping.   10

LOCKIT.

But I don't see any article of the jewels.

---

1. *Coronation account*] (1) the account of items stolen during the coronation
of George II, three months before *The Beggar's Opera* opened, (2) or, by
implication, the large civil list secured by Walpole for George II, whereby
Walpole kept control over the government. See J. H. Plumb, *Sir Robert
Walpole, the King's Minister* (Boston, 1961), pp. 168 f.
5. *installments*] An installment was "the action of installing or fact of
being installed; formal induction into an office or dignity; installation"
(*OED*), with specific reference here to the annual installations of the Lord
Mayor of London. Peachum's speech (ll. 3–5) therefore means approxi-
mately this: from payments made by Peachum to the gang for stolen
goods, the Coronation netted the gang more than could have been gained
from thefts at ten Lord Mayor's Days.
7. *tail*] train.

PEACHUM.

Those are so well known that they must be sent abroad.
You'll find them entered under the article of exportation.
As for the snuffboxes, watches, swords, etc., I thought it best
to enter them under their several heads.   15

LOCKIT.

"Seven and twenty women's pockets complete," with the
several things therein contained; all sealed, numbered, and
entered.

PEACHUM.

But, brother, it is impossible for us now to enter upon this
affair. We should have the whole day before us. Besides, the   20
account of the last half year's plate is in a book by itself,
which lies at the other office.

LOCKIT [to a servant].

Bring us then more liquor. [To Peachum.] Today shall
be for pleasure, tomorrow for business.

[The liquor is served. They drink.]

Ah, brother, those daughters of ours are two slippery   25
hussies. Keep a watchful eye upon Polly, and Macheath
in a day or two shall be our own again.

AIR XLV, Down in the North Country, etc.

What gudgeons are we men!
    Ev'ry woman's easy prey.
Though we have felt the hook, again   30
    We bite, and they betray.

The bird that hath been trapped,
    When he hears his calling mate,
To her he flies, again he's clapped
    Within the wiry grate.   35

27.1. etc.] O1–2; om. Q.

---

12. Those . . . abroad] Jonathan Wild controlled a smuggling operation
by which he sent goods abroad that could not safely be sold in England.
He also controlled the foreign sale through his own agents (Wild, p. 286).
16. pockets] small bags, coin purses.
34. clapped] a pun: (1) thrown, (2) infected by a venereal disease.

PEACHUM.

But what signifies catching the bird, if your daughter
Lucy will set open the door of the cage?

LOCKIT.

If men were answerable for the follies and frailties of
their wives and daughters, no friends could keep a good
correspondence together for two days. This is unkind of 40
you, brother; for among good friends, what they say or do
goes for nothing.

Enter a Servant.

SERVANT.

Sir, here's Mrs. Diana Trapes wants to speak with you.

PEACHUM.

Shall we admit her, Brother Lockit?

LOCKIT.

By all means. She's a good customer, and a fine-spoken 45
woman. And a woman who drinks and talks so freely will
enliven the conversation.

PEACHUM.

Desire her to walk in.   *Exit* Servant.

[III.vi]   Peachum, Lockit. [*To them enter*] Mrs. Trapes.

PEACHUM.

Dear Mrs. Di, your servant. [*He kisses her.*]   One may
know by your kiss that your gin is excellent.

MRS. TRAPES.

I was always very curious in my liquors.

LOCKIT.

There is no perfumed breath like it. [*He kisses her also.*]   I
have been long acquainted with the flavor of those lips,   5
han't I, Mrs. Di?

[*He offers her a glass.*]

MRS. TRAPES.

Fill it up.

[*He pours the drink.*]

I take as large draughts of liquor, as I did of love.

[*She takes the drink and drains it quickly.*]

I hate a flincher in either.

-67-

AIR XLVI, *A Shepherd Kept Sheep, etc.*

In the days of my youth I could bill like a dove, fa, la, la, etc.   10
Like a sparrow at all times was ready for love, fa, la, la, etc.
The life of all mortals in kissing should pass,
Lip to lip while we're young, then the lip to the glass, fa, etc.

But now, Mr. Peachum, to our business. If you have blacks
of any kind, brought in of late—manteaus, velvet scarfs,   15
petticoats—let it be what it will, I am your chap; for all
my ladies are very fond of mourning.

PEACHUM.

Why, look ye, Mrs. Di, you deal so hard with us that we
can afford to give the gentlemen who venture their lives
for the goods little or nothing.   20

MRS. TRAPES.

The hard times oblige me to go very near in my dealing.
To be sure, of late years I have been a great sufferer by
the parliament. Three thousand pounds would hardly make
me amends. The act for destroying the Mint was a severe
cut upon our business. Till then, if a customer stepped   25
out of the way, we knew where to have her. No doubt you
know Mrs. Coaxer. There's a wench now (till today) with
a good suit of clothes of mine upon her back, and I could
never set eyes upon her for three months together. Since
the act too against imprisonment for small sums, my loss   30
there too hath been very considerable, and it must be so,
when a lady can borrow a handsome petticoat, or a clean

---

13. fa, etc.] *O1–2*; fa, la, etc. *Q*.

---

17. *fond of mourning*] because their sweethearts have been recently
hanged.

24. *act . . . Mint*] Three statutes had been passed outlawing the Mint's
status as a sanctuary. These were 8 and 9 William III, c.27; 9 Geo. I,
c.29; and 11 Geo. I, c.22. Mrs. Trapes is apparently referring to the recent
statutes, which had been effective (Pennant, p. 40).

30. *act . . . sums*] an act passed in 1725 (12 Geo. I, c.29) which was
designed to prevent arrests for indebtedness below ten pounds (if the case
was to be tried in the superior courts) or forty shillings (if in the inferior
courts). Mrs. Trapes's complaint is not well founded, however, for this
statute, like many which followed it, was ineffective, and it was not until
well into the nineteenth century that imprisonment for debt, small and
large, was abolished (Holdsworth, pp. 595, 600).

gown, and I not have the least hank upon her! And o' my conscience, nowadays most ladies take a delight in cheating, when they can do it with safety.   35

PEACHUM.

Madam, you had a handsome gold watch of us t'other day for seven guineas. Considering we must have our profit, to a gentleman upon the road, a gold watch will be scarce worth the taking.

MRS. TRAPES.

Consider, Mr. Peachum, that watch was remarkable, and   40 not of very safe sale. If you have any black velvet scarfs, they are a handsome winter wear, and take with most gentlemen who deal with my customers. 'Tis I that put the ladies upon a good foot. 'Tis not youth or beauty that fixes their price. The gentlemen always pay according to their   45 dress, from half a crown to two guineas; and yet those hussies make nothing of bilking of me. Then too, allowing for accidents—I have eleven fine customers now down under the surgeon's hands. What with fees and other expenses, there are great goings-out, and no comings-in, and not a   50 farthing to pay for at least a month's clothing. We run great risks, great risks indeed.

PEACHUM.

As I remember, you said something just now of Mrs. Coaxer.

MRS. TRAPES.

Yes, sir. To be sure I stripped her of a suit of my own   55 clothes about two hours ago; and have left her as she should be, in her shift, with a lover of hers at my house. She called him upstairs as he was going to Marybone in a hackney-coach. And I hope, for her own sake and mine, she will persuade the Captain to redeem her, for the Captain   60 is very generous to the ladies.

LOCKIT.

What captain?

MRS. TRAPES.

He thought I did not know him. An intimate acquaintance of yours, Mr. Peachum, only Captain Macheath, as fine as a lord.   65

---

33. *hank*] hold, claim.

PEACHUM.

Tomorrow, dear Mrs. Di, you shall set your own price upon any of the goods you like. We have at least half a dozen velvet scarfs, and all at your service. Will you give me leave to make you a present of this suit of nightclothes for your own wearing? But are you sure it is Captain Macheath? 70

MRS. TRAPES.

Though he thinks I have forgot him, nobody knows him better. I have taken a great deal of the Captain's money in my time at second hand, for he always loved to have his ladies well dressed.

PEACHUM.

Mr. Lockit and I have a little business with the Captain. 75 You understand me. And we will satisfy you for Mrs. Coaxer's debt.

LOCKIT.

Depend upon it. We will deal like men of honor.

MRS. TRAPES.

I don't inquire after your affairs. So whatever happens, I wash my hands on't. It hath always been my maxim, that 80 one friend should assist another. But if you please, I'll take one of the scarfs home with me. 'Tis always good to have something in hand. [*Exeunt.*]

[III.vii]   *Scene, Newgate.*
                         Lucy [*alone*].

LUCY.

Jealousy, rage, love, and fear are at once tearing me to pieces. How I am weather-beaten and shattered with distresses!

AIR XLVII, *One Evening Having Lost My Way, etc.*

I'm like a skiff on the ocean tossed,
　　Now high, now low, with each billow born[e],   5
With her rudder broke, and her anchor lost,
　　Deserted and all forlorn.
While thus I lie rolling and tossing all night,

3.1. *etc.*] *O1–2; om. Q.*

That Polly lies sporting on seas of delight!
    Revenge, revenge, revenge,   10
Shall appease my restless sprite.

I have the ratsbane ready. I run no risk, for I can lay her
death upon the gin, and so many die of that naturally that
I shall never be called in question. But say I were to be
hanged, I never could be hanged for anything that would   15
give me greater comfort than the poisoning that slut.

Enter Filch.

FILCH.

Madam, here's our Miss Polly come to wait upon you.

LUCY.

Show her in.   [*Exit* Filch.]

[III.viii]   Lucy. [*To her enter*] Polly.

LUCY.

Dear madam, your servant. I hope you will pardon my
passion when I was so happy to see you last. I was so over-
run with the spleen that I was perfectly out of myself. And
really, when one hath the spleen, everything is to be
excused by a friend.   5

AIR XLVIII, *Now Roger, I'll Tell Thee, Because Thou'rt
My Son*

When a wife's in her pout
(As she's sometimes, no doubt)
    The good husband as meek as a lamb,
      Her vapors to still,
      First grants her her will,   10
    And the quieting draught is a dram.
Poor man! And the quieting draught is a dram.

I wish all our quarrels might have so comfortable a
reconciliation.

---

13. *so . . . naturally*] Gin was cheap and plentiful, and Londoners consumed
it in great quantities. Social commentators at the time recognized the wide
consumption as a danger to public health, particularly among the poor.
[III.viii]

3, 4, 9. *spleen, vapors*] fashionable terms describing and excusing ill
humor, with a remote basis in psychosomatic theory.

POLLY.

I have no excuse for my own behavior, madam, but my 15
misfortunes. And really, madam, I suffer too upon your
account.

LUCY.

But, Miss Polly, in the way of friendship, will you give me
leave to propose a glass of cordial to you?

POLLY.

Strong waters are apt to give me the headache. I hope, 20
madam, you will excuse me.

LUCY.

Not the greatest lady in the land could have better in
her closet, for her own private drinking. You seem mighty
low in spirits, my dear.

POLLY.

I am sorry, madam, my health will not allow me to accept 25
of your offer. I should not have left you in the rude manner
I did when we met last, madam, had not my papa hauled
me away so unexpectedly. I was indeed somewhat provoked,
and perhaps might use some expressions that were dis-
respectful. But really, madam, the Captain treated me 30
with so much contempt and cruelty that I deserved your
pity rather than your resentment.

LUCY.

But since his escape, no doubt all matters are made up
again. Ah Polly, Polly, 'tis I am the unhappy wife, and
he loves you as if you were only his mistress. 35

POLLY.

Sure, madam, you cannot think me so happy as to be the
object of your jealousy. A man is always afraid of a woman
who loves him too well, so that I must expect to be neglected
and avoided.

LUCY.

Then our cases, my dear Polly, are exactly alike. Both of us 40
indeed have been too fond.

AIR XLIX, *Oh Bessy Bell*

POLLY.   A curse attends that woman's love
                    Who always would be pleasing.

41.1. *Bell*] *O1–2*; Bell, etc. *Q*.

LUCY.   The pertness of the billing dove,
               Like tickling, is but teasing.   45
POLLY.   What then in love can woman do?
LUCY.   If we grow fond they shun us.
POLLY.   And when we fly them, they pursue,
LUCY.   But leave us when they've won us.
LUCY.

Love is so very whimsical in both sexes that it is impossible   50
to be lasting. But my heart is particular, and contradicts
my own observation.

POLLY.

But really, Mistress Lucy, by his last behavior I think
I ought to envy you. When I was forced from him, he did
not show the least tenderness. But perhaps he hath a heart   55
not capable of it.

AIR L, *Would Fate to Me Belinda Give*

Among the men, coquets we find,
Who court by turns all womankind;
And we grant all their hearts desired,
When they are flattered and admired.   60

The coquets of both sexes are self-lovers, and that is a love no
other whatever can dispossess. I fear, my dear Lucy, our
husband is one of those.

LUCY.

Away with these melancholy reflections. Indeed, my dear
Polly, we are both of us a cup too low. Let me prevail   65
upon you to accept of my offer.

AIR LI, *Come, Sweet Lass, etc.*

Come, sweet lass,
Let's banish sorrow
Till tomorrow;
Come, sweet lass,   70
Let's take a chirping glass.
Wine can clear
The vapors of despair,

66.1. *etc.*] *O1–2*; *om. Q*.

51. *particular*] (1) special, unique, different, (2) partial to only one man.

And make us light as air;
Then drink, and banish care.   75

I can't bear, child, to see you in such low spirits. And I
must persuade you to what I know will do you good.
(*Aside.*) I shall now soon be even with the hypocritical
strumpet.   [*Exit* Lucy.]

[III.ix]   Polly [*alone*].

POLLY.

All this wheedling of Lucy cannot be for nothing. At this
time too, when I know she hates me. The dissembling of a
woman is always the forerunner of mischief. By pouring
strong waters down my throat, she thinks to pump some
secrets out of me. I'll be upon my guard, and won't taste a   5
drop of her liquor, I'm resolved.

[III.x]   Polly. [*Enter to her*] Lucy, *with strong waters.*

LUCY [*offering* Polly *a glass*].
    Come, Miss Polly.
POLLY [*refusing it*].
    Indeed, child, you have given yourself trouble to no purpose.
    You must, my dear, excuse me.
LUCY.
    Really, Miss Polly, you are so squeamishly affected about
    taking a cup of strong waters, as a lady before company. I   5
    vow, Polly, I shall take it monstrously ill if you refuse
    me. Brandy and men (though women love them never so
    well) are always taken by us with some reluctance, unless
    'tis in private.
POLLY [*accepting the glass*].
    I protest, madam, it goes against me. —What do I see?   10
    Macheath again in custody! —Now every glimmering of
    happiness is lost.   *Drops the glass of liquor on the ground.*
LUCY (*aside*).
    Since things are thus, I'm glad the wench hath escaped, for

[III.x]
0.1. Polly . . . *waters*] Lucy,   *with*   13. S.D. *aside*] *O1*; *om. O2, Q.*
Strong-Waters. Polly. *O1–2, Q.*

by this event, 'tis plain she was not happy enough to
deserve to be poisoned.   15

[III.xi]
Lucy, Polly. [*Enter to them*] Lockit [*and*] Peachum, [*with*] Macheath
[*in custody.*]

LOCKIT.

Set your heart to rest, Captain. You have neither the
chance of love or money for another escape, for you are
ordered to be called down upon your trial immediately.

PEACHUM.

Away, hussies! This is not a time for a man to be hampered
with his wives. You see, the gentleman is in chains already.   5

LUCY.

Oh husband, husband, my heart longed to see thee; but to
see thee thus distracts me!

POLLY.

Will not my dear husband look upon his Polly? Why
hadst thou not flown to me for protection? With me thou
hadst been safe.   10

AIR LII, *The Last Time I Went O'er the Moor*

POLLY.   Hither, dear husband, turn your eyes.
LUCY.   Bestow one glance to cheer me.
POLLY.   Think with that look, thy Polly dies.
LUCY.   Oh shun me not, but hear me.
POLLY.   'Tis Polly sues.
LUCY   'Tis Lucy speaks.   15
POLLY.   Is thus true love requited?
LUCY.   My heart is bursting.
POLLY.   Mine too breaks.
LUCY.   Must I,
POLLY.   Must I be slighted?

MACHEATH.

What would you have me say, ladies? You see, this affair
will soon be at an end, without my disobliging either of you.   20

0.1–2. *Lucy . . . custody*]   Lockit,   *O1–2, Q*.
Macheath, Peachum, Lucy, Polly

PEACHUM.

But the settling this point, Captain, might prevent a
lawsuit between your two widows.

AIR LIII, *Tom Tinker's My True Love*

MACHEATH.

Which way shall I turn me? How can I decide?
Wives, the day of our death, are as fond as a bride.
One wife is too much for most husbands to hear,   25
But two at a time there's no mortal can bear.
This way, and that way, and which way I will,
What would comfort the one, t'other wife would take ill.

POLLY.

But if his own misfortunes have made him insensible to
mine, a father sure will be more compassionate. [*She goes*   30
to Peachum.]   Dear, dear sir, sink the material evidence,
and bring him off at his trial. [*Kneeling.*]   Polly upon her
knees begs it of you.

AIR LIV, *I Am a Poor Shepherd Undone*

When my hero in court appears,
   And stands arraigned for his life,   35
Then think of poor Polly's tears;
   For ah! Poor Polly's his wife.
Like the sailor he holds up his hand,
   Distressed on the dashing wave.
To die a dry death at land   40
   Is as bad as a wat'ry grave.
And alas, poor Polly!
Alack, and welladay!
Before I was in love,
   Oh! Every month was May.   45

LUCY [*going to* Lockit].

If Peachum's heart is hardened, sure you, sir, will have more
compassion on a daughter. I know the evidence is in your
power. How then can you be a tyrant to me?   *Kneeling.*

22.1. *Love*] *O1–2*; Love, etc. *Q.*

31–32. *sink ... trial*] i.e., order the principal "witnesses" against
Macheath not to testify, and get him an alibi.

AIR LV, *Ianthe the Lovely, etc.*

When he holds up his hand arraigned for his life,
Oh think of your daughter, and think I'm his wife!   50
What are cannons, or bombs, or clashing of swords?
For death is more certain by witnesses' words.
Then nail up their lips; that dread thunder allay;
And each month of my life will hereafter be May.

LOCKIT.

Macheath's time is come, Lucy. We know our own affairs;   55
therefore let us have no more whimpering or whining.

AIR LVI, *A Cobbler There Was, etc.*

Ourselves, like the great, to secure a retreat,
When matters require it, must give up our gang;
    And good reason why,
    Or, instead of the fry,   60
    Ev'n Peachum and I,
Like poor petty rascals, might hang, hang;
Like poor petty rascals, might hang.

PEACHUM.

Set your heart at rest, Polly. Your husband is to die today.
Therefore, if you are not already provided, 'tis high time   65
to look about for another. There's comfort for you, you slut.

LOCKIT.

We are ready, sir, to conduct you to the Old Bailey.

AIR LVII, *Bonny Dundee*

MACHEATH.

    The charge is prepared; the lawyers are met;
    The judges all ranged (a terrible show!).
    I go, undismayed, for death is a debt,   70
    A debt on demand, so take what I owe.
    Then farewell, my love—dear charmers, adieu.
    Contented I die. 'Tis the better for you.
    Here ends all dispute the rest of our lives,
    For this way at once I please all my wives.   75

Now, gentlemen, I am ready to attend you.
          [*Exeunt* Macheath, Lockit, *and* Peachum.]

56.1–63. AIR LVI . . . might hang]   *copies of O1.*
O2, Q, some copies of O1; om. *some*

[III.xii]   Lucy, Polly. [*To them enter*] Filch.

POLLY.

Follow them, Filch, to the court. And when the trial is
over, bring me a particular account of his behavior,
and of everything that happened. You'll find me here with
Miss Lucy.   *Ex*[*it*] Filch.

[*Orchestra begins playing.*]

But why all this music?   5

LUCY.

The prisoners whose trials are put off till next session are
diverting themselves.

POLLY.

Sure there is nothing so charming as music. I'm fond
of it to distraction. But alas! Now, all mirth seems an
insult upon my affliction. Let us retire, my dear Lucy,   10
and indulge our sorrows. The noisy crew, you see, are
coming upon us.   *Exeunt.*

A dance of prisoners in chains, etc.

[III.xiii]   *The condemned hold.*

Macheath [*alone*], *in a melancholy posture.*

AIR LVIII, *Happy Groves*

Oh cruel, cruel, cruel case!
Must I suffer this disgrace?

AIR LIX, *Of All the Girls That Are So Smart*

Of all the friends in time of grief,
    When threat'ning Death looks grimmer,
Not one so sure can bring relief,   5
    As this best friend, a brimmer.   *Drinks.*

AIR LX, *Britons Strike Home*

Since I must swing, I scorn, I scorn to wince or whine.   *Rises.*

AIR LXI, *Chevy Chase*

But now again my spirits sink;
I'll raise them high with wine.

                              Drinks a glass of wine.

AIR LXII, *To Old Sir Simon the King*

But valor the stronger grows,   10
  The stronger liquor we're drinking.
And how can we feel our woes,
  When we've lost the trouble of thinking?   *Drinks.*

AIR LXIII, *Joy to Great Caesar*

  If thus— A man can die
  Much bolder with brandy.   15
    Pours out a bumper of brandy.

AIR LXIV, *There was an Old Woman*

So I drink off this bumper. —And now I can stand the test,
And my comrades shall see that I die as brave as the best.
                           Drinks.

AIR LXV, *Did You Ever Hear of a Gallant Sailor*

  But can I leave my pretty hussies,
  Without one tear, or tender sigh?

AIR LXVI, *Why Are Mine Eyes Still Flowing*

  Their eyes, their lips, their busses   20
  Recall my love— Ah, must I die?

AIR LXVII, *Greensleeves*

Since laws were made for ev'ry degree,
To curb vice in others, as well as me,
I wonder we han't better company
  Upon Tyburn tree!   25
But gold from law can take out the sting;
And if rich men, like us, were to swing,
'Twould thin the land, such numbers to string
  Upon Tyburn tree!

        [*Enter a* Jailer.]

JAILER.

  Some friends of yours, Captain, desire to be admitted. I   30
leave you together.   [*Exit.*]

15.2. *Woman*] *O1–2*; Woman, etc.
Q.

[III.xiv]

Macheath. [*To him enter*] Ben Budge [*and*] Matt of the Mint.

MACHEATH.

For my having broke prison, you see, gentlemen, I am
ordered immediate execution. The sheriff's officers, I
believe, are now at the door. —That Jemmy Twitcher
should peach me, I own surprised me. 'Tis a plain proof
that the world is all alike, and that even our gang can no   5
more trust one another than other people. Therefore, I beg
you, gentlemen, look well to yourselves, for in all probability
you may live some months longer.

MATT OF THE MINT.

We are heartily sorry, Captain, for your misfortune. But
'tis what we must all come to.   10

MACHEATH.

Peachum and Lockit, you know, are infamous scoundrels.
Their lives are as much in your power as yours are in theirs.
Remember your dying friend! 'Tis my last request. Bring
those villains to the gallows before you, and I am satisfied.

MATT OF THE MINT.

We'll do't.   15

[*Enter the* Jailer.]

JAILER.

Miss Polly and Miss Lucy entreat a word with you.

MACHEATH.

Gentlemen, adieu.   [*Exeunt* Ben Budge *and* Matt of the Mint.]

[III.xv]   Macheath. [*To him enter*] Lucy [*and*] Polly.

MACHEATH.

My dear Lucy, my dear Polly, whatsoever hath passed
between us is now at an end. If you are fond of marrying

[III.xv]
0.1. Macheath . . . Polly] Lucy,
Macheath, Polly *O1–2*, *Q*.

[III.xvi]
3–4. *That . . . me*] For Hogarth's scene of a rogue impeaching his accom-
plice, see Plate X of *Industry and Idleness*.

again, the best advice I can give you is to ship yourselves
off for the West Indies, where you'll have a fair chance of
getting a husband apiece, or by good luck two or three, as   5
you like best.

POLLY.
How can I support this sight!

LUCY.
There is nothing moves one so much as a great man in distress.

AIR LXVIII, *All You That Must Take a Leap*, etc.

LUCY.   Would I might be hanged!
POLLY.   And I would so too!   10
LUCY.   To be hanged with you,
POLLY   My dear, with you.
MACHEATH.   Oh leave me to thought. I fear. I doubt.
                   I tremble. I droop. (*Turns up the empty bottle.*) See,
                      my courage is out.
POLLY.   No token of love?
MACHEATH.   (*Turns up the empty pot.*) See, my courage is out.
LUCY.   No token of love?
POLLY.   Adieu.
LUCY.   Farewell.   15

[*Bell begins tolling.*]

MACHEATH.   But hark! I hear the toll of the bell.
CHORUS.   Tol de rol lol, etc.

[*Enter the* Jailer.]

JAILER.
Four women more, Captain, with a child apiece! See, here
they come.

Enter women and children.

MACHEATH.
What—four wives more! This is too much. —Here— tell   20
the Sheriff's officers I am ready.   *Exit* Macheath *guarded.*

---

16. *toll of the bell*] The bell of St. Sepulchre's church, next door to Newgate Prison, customarily began ringing five minutes before condemned
criminals were to be driven to Tyburn. (Pennant, pp. 286–238; Smith,
xvii f.).

[III.xvi]   *To them, enter* Player *and* Beggar.

PLAYER.

But, honest friend, I hope you don't intend that Macheath
shall be really executed.

BEGGAR.

Most certainly, sir. To make the piece perfect, I was for
doing strict poetical justice. Macheath is to be hanged; and
for the other personages of the drama, the audience must   5
have supposed they were all either hanged or transported.

PLAYER.

Why then, friend, this is a downright deep tragedy. The
catastrophe is manifestly wrong, for an opera must end
happily.

BEGGAR.

Your objection, sir, is very just, and is easily removed.   10
For you must allow that in this kind of drama 'tis no matter
how absurdly things are brought about. —So, you rabble
there, run and cry a reprieve. Let the prisoner be brought
back to his wives in triumph.

            [*Cries of "Reprieve!"*]

PLAYER.

All this we must do, to comply with the taste of the town.   15

BEGGAR.

Through the whole piece you may observe such a similitude
of manners in high and low life, that it is difficult to determine whether (in the fashionable vices) the fine gentlemen
imitate the gentlemen of the road, or the gentlemen of
the road the fine gentlemen. Had the play remained as I   20
at first intended, it would have carried a most excellent
moral. 'Twould have shown that the lower sort of people
have their vices in a degree as well as the rich, and that
they are punished for them.

[III.xvii]   *To them [enter]* Macheath *with rabble, etc.*

MACHEATH.

So, it seems, I am not left to my choice, but must have a
wife at last. [*To the women.*] Look ye, my dears, we will

have no controversy now. Let us give this day to mirth, and
I am sure she who thinks herself my wife will testify her joy
by a dance.   5

ALL.

Come, a dance, a dance.

MACHEATH.

Ladies, I hope you will give me leave to present a partner
to each of you. And (if I may without offense) for this time,
I take Polly for mine.   [*To* Polly.]   And for life, you slut,
for we were really married.   [*To the other ladies.*]   As for the   10
rest—   (*To* Polly.)   But at present keep your own secret.

A Dance.

AIR, LXIX, *Lumps of Pudding, etc.*

MACHEATH.

Thus I stand like the Turk, with his doxies around;
From all sides their glances his passion confound;
For black, brown, and fair, his inconstancy burns,
And the different beauties subdue him by turns: 15
Each calls forth her charms, to provoke his desires;
Though willing to all, with but one he retires.
But think of this maxim, and put off your sorrow:
The wretch of today may be happy tomorrow.

CHORUS.   But think of this maxim, etc.   [*Exeunt.*]   20

FINIS

18. your] *O1–2, Q*; all *Q* (*in* "*Songs
in 'The Beggar's Opera'*").

Appendix A

The Music of *The Beggar's Opera*
with Keyboard Accompaniments
Realized from the Basses of
John Christopher Pepusch by Edward Smith

This version of the songs in *The Beggar's Opera* is intended primarily as a reader's edition. It is not a performing edition, which would have to take into account problems of transposition, orchestration, additional music, etc. (some of these problems are discussed by Edward J. Dent in his frankly modern version, *The Beggar's Opera* [London: Oxford University Press, 1954], pp. iii–ix). The music included here is taken from the "Songs in *The Beggar's Opera*," a section which takes up the last thirty-eight pages of Q. These versions were prepared by Dr. Pepusch, and hence they offer the best authority for how the songs were performed at Lincoln's Inn Fields. Occasionally the fitting of song to tune requires a slight divergence from the O1 copy text, as in Air LXVIII, where certain lines are repeated although the repetition is not indicated in the copy-text. The music sometimes requires that the modernized spelling of words and phrases like *flower*, *every*, and *To your* be contracted (as *flow'r*, *ev'ry*, and *T'your*); variations of this kind have been made silently. The forms of words in the copy-text have been preferred to those in the "Songs in *The Beggar's Opera*" in Q. Thus, the "Songs" prints "Ho ho ra in ambora" in Air XXXIX, but this form is replaced by "Oh, oh ray, oh Amborah" from the copy-text.

The titles of the tunes are those used by Gay, and the versions of the tunes are unquestionably the ones he used. As a result, some of the tunes presented here differ widely from what are to us more familiar versions (Air LXVII, "Greensleeves," for example). Gay adapted others (e.g., Airs XX and XLI) from airs by such well-known composers as Purcell and Handel; Pepusch set the airs to simpler harmonies, as befits the general "popular" style of the work.

The Music of "The Beggar's Opera"

It has not been the aim in this edition to supply either "authentic" versions of the tunes or extensive historical commentaries; nor has it been the aim to list alternate titles by which the tunes were known. Original texts, variants, alternate titles, and commentaries may be found in the sources listed in the "Note on the Origins of the Tunes in *The Beggar's Opera*" on pages xxviii f. of this book. The somewhat rudimentary basses provided by Pepusch have been left substantially intact, in spite of occasional crudities. In the few places where the given bass seemed impossible, the original is always presented in a footnote. The accompaniments supplied here are intended to suggest those which a reasonably competent eighteenth-century musician might have played while reading through the songs. Obviously, many of the tunes would benefit from a more sensitive, sophisticated harmonization than that implied by Pepusch's basses (a comparison of Purcell's and Handel's originals with Pepusch's simplified versions in *The Beggar's Opera* is instructive on this point). But, in keeping with the "low-life" subject matter of the work, Pepusch undoubtedly suppressed the temptation to provide anything more than the simplest framework for tunes that could be heard on any street corner.

The overture has been arranged for keyboard from the open score, with indications of the original instrumentation. The dotted rhythms of the first half have been more precisely notated. Key signatures have been modernized where necessary, and obvious mistakes corrected without comment. All other editorial additions and corrections are enclosed within brackets. No dynamic or tempo markings have been added to the songs; these will be suggested by Gay's vivid text.

EDWARD SMITH

New York City, April, 1968

Overture

Composed by Dr. Pepusch

An Old Woman Clothed in Gray

AIR I

anon.

cheat;_____ The law-yer be-knaves the di - vine;_____ And the states-man, be-cause he's so great, Thinks his trade as hon-est as mine.

The Bonny Gray-Eyed Morn

AIR II

Jeremiah Clarke

FILCH

'Tis wom-an that se-du-ces__ all__ man-kind, By her we first were taught the__ wheed-ling__ arts; Her ver-y eyes can cheat; when most she's kind, She tricks us__ of our mon-ey with our hearts. For

her, like wolves by night, we roam for— prey, And prac-tice ev'-ry

fraud to bribe her— charms; For suits of love, like law, are

won by— pay, And beau-ty— must be fee'd in-to— our arms.

Cold and Raw

AIR III

anon.

fit but a cord (A rope so charm-ing a zone is!), The youth in his

cart hath the air of a lord, And we cry, "There dies an A-don - is!"

Why Is Your Faithful Slave Disdained?

AIR IV

Giovanni Battista Buononcini

made   a   wife,   Her hon-or's   singed,   and then for

life,   She's   what   I   dare not   name.

Of All the Simple Things We Do

AIR V

anon.

MRS. PEACHUM

A maid is like the gold - en ore, Which hath guin-eas in-trin-si-cal

in't,_____ Whose worth is nev - er known be-fore It is tried and im-

- pressed in the mint._____ A__ wife's like a guin-ea in gold,_____

Stamped with the name of her spouse,_____ Now here, now there, is bought, or is sold, And is cur - rent in ev - er - y house._____

What Shall I Do to Show How Much I Love Her

AIR VI

Henry Purcell

Vir - gins are like the fair flow'r__ in__ its__ lus - - ter,

Which in the gar-den e - na - mels the ground; Near it the

bees in play flut - ter__ and__ clus - - ter, And gaud-y

but-ter - flies frol - ic a - round.   But, when once plucked, 'tis no

long-er al - lur - ing, To Cov-ent Gar-den 'tis — sent — (as   yet

sweet),   There fades, and shrinks, and grows past all — en -

- dur - ing, Rots, stinks, and dies, and is— trod und - er feet.

Oh London Is a Fine Town

AIR VII

anon.

MRS. PEACHUM (*in a very great passion*)

Our Pol - ly is a sad slut, nor heeds what we have taught her.

[Fine]

I won-der an-y man a-live will ev-er rear a daugh-ter! For

she must have both hoods and gowns, and hoops to swell her pride, With

Grim King of the Ghosts

AIR VIII   *anon.*

POLLY

Can love be con-trolled by ad-vice? Will Cu-pid our moth-ers o-bey? Though my heart were as fro-zen as ice, At his flame 'twould have melt-ed a-way. When he kissed me so close-ly he pressed, 'Twas so

sweet that I must have com-plied; So I thought it both

saf-est and best To mar-ry, for fear you should chide

Oh Jenny, Oh Jenny, Where Hast Thou Been

AIR IX *anon.*

MRS. PEACHUM

Oh Pol - ly, you might have toyed and kissed. By keep-ing men off, you keep them on.

POLLY

But he so teas-ed me, And he so pleased me, What I did, you must have done.

Thomas, I Cannot

AIR X

anon.

du - ty's___ paid. Oh joy be - yond ex - pres - sion! Thus,

safe a - shore, I ask___ no more, My all is in my pos-

- ses - sion, pos - ses - sion, My all is in my pos - ses - sion. ___

A Soldier and a Sailor

AIR XI

John Eccles

A fox may steal your hens, sir, A whore your health and pence, sir, Your

daugh-ter rob your chest, sir, Your wife may steal your rest, sir, A

thief your goods and plate,

A

thief__ your goods and plate._____ But this__ is all but

pick - ing, With rest, pence, chest, and chick - en; It

ev - er was__ de - creed, sir,__ If law - yer's hand is__

Now Ponder Well, Ye Parents Dear

AIR XII

anon.

Oh, pon-der well! Be not se - vere; So save a wretch-ed wife!   For

on the rope   that hangs my dear   De - pends poor Pol - ly's life.

Le Printemps Rappelle aux Armes

AIR XIII

anon.

The tur - tle thus with plain - tive cry - ing, Her lov - er dy - ing, The tur - tle thus with plain - tive cry - ing La - ments her dove. Down she drops____ quite spent__ with

sigh - ing,   Paired   in death, as_____ paired in   love.

Pretty Parrot, Say

AIR XIV

John Freeman

MACHEATH

Pret-ty Pol-ly, say, When I— was a - way, Did your fan-cy nev-er

stray To some new-er lov - er?   With-out dis - guise,— Heav-ing

POLLY

sighs, Dot-ing eyes,—   My con-stant heart dis-cov - er.   Fond -

- ly let___ me loll! Fond - ly let___ me loll! Oh pret-ty, pret-ty___ Poll.

Pray, Fair One, Be Kind

AIR XV

Richard Leveridge

MACHEATH

My heart was so free, It roved like the bee, Till Pol-ly my pas-sion re-

-quit-ed; I sipped each flow'r, I changed ev'-ry hour, I

sipped each flow'r, I changed ev'-ry hour, But here ev'-ry flow'r is u-ni-ted.

Over the Hills and Far Away

AIR XVI

anon.

MACHEATH

Were I ___ laid on Green-land's coast, And in ___ my ___ arms em-braced my lass, Warm a - midst e - ter - nal frost, Too soon the ___ half year's night would pass.

POLLY

Were I ___ sold on ___

POLLY

MACHEATH

Ev' - ry night would kiss and play, If with me you'd

POLLY

fond - ly stray Ov - er the hills and far a - way.

Gin Thou Wert Mine Awn Thing

AIR XVII

anon.

POLLY

Oh what pain it is to— part! Can I— leave thee, can I— leave thee?

Oh what pain it is to— part! Can thy Pol - ly ev - er—

leave thee? But lest death my love should thwart, And

bring thee to the fa - tal_ cart, Thus I tear_ thee from_ my
bleed - ing heart! Fly hence,_ and let_ me_ leave_ thee.

Oh, the Broom

AIR XVIII

anon.

1. MACHEATH; 2. POLLY

1. The mis - er thus a shil - ling__ sees, Which he's ob - liged__ to__ pay, With sighs re - signs it__ by de - grees, And fears 'tis__ gone for__ aye.

2. The boy, thus, when his spar - row's__ flown, the__ bird in__ si - lence eyes; But soon as__ out__ of__ sight 'tis__ gone, Whines, whim-pers, sobs, and cries.

Fill Ev'ry Glass

AIR XIX

anon.

1. MATT; 2. CHORUS

Fill ev'-ry glass, for wine in-spires us, And fires us With cour-age, love, and joy. Wom-en and wine should life em--ploy. Is there aught else on earth de-sir - - ous?

March in *Rinaldo*, with Drums and Trumpets

AIR XX

G. F. Handel

MATT

Let us take the road. Hark! I hear the sound of coach-es! The

hour of at-tack ap - proach - es, T'your arms, brave boys, and load.

See the ball I hold! Let the chy - mists toil like as - ses, Our

fire their fire sur - pas - ses, And turns all__ our lead to gold.

Would You Have a Young Virgin

AIR XXI

Thomas D'Urfey

MACHEATH

If the heart of a man is de-pressed with cares, The mist is dis-pelled when a wo-man ap-pears; Like the notes of a fid-dle, she sweet-ly, sweet-ly Rais-es the spir-its and

charms our ears.   Ros - es and lil - ies her cheeks dis-close,

But her ripe lips are more sweet than those.   Press her, Ca-ress her; With

bliss - es, Her kiss - es Dis-solve us in pleas-ure, and soft.   re - pose.

Cotillon

AIR XXII

anon.

MACHEATH

Youth's the sea-son made for— joys; Love is then our du-ty;

She a-lone who that em-ploys Well de-serves her beau-ty.

Let's be— gay While we— may; Beau-ty's a flow-er des-

CHORUS

-pised in de-cay. Youth's the sea-son made for joys;

Love is then our du - ty. Let us drink and sport to - day;

Ours is not to-mor - row. Love with youth flies swift a - way;

Age is nought but__ sor - row. Dance and__ sing; Time's on the

wing; Life nev-er knows the re - turn__ of__ spring.

CHORUS

Let us drink and sport to - day; Ours is not to - mor - row.

All in a Misty Morning

AIR XXIII

anon.

JENNY DIVER

Be - fore the barn-door crow-ing, The cock by hens at-tend - ed, His

eyes a - round him throw - ing, Stands for a while sus - pend - ed. Then

one he sing-les from the crew, And cheers the hap-py hen, With

When Once I Lay with Another Man's Wife

AIR XXIV

anon.

JENNY DIVER

The game-sters and law-yers are jug-glers a-like; If they med-dle your all is in dan - ger. Like gyp-sies, if once they can fing-er a souse, Your pock-ets they pick, and they

pil - fer   your house,   And give your es - tate to   a   stran - ger.

When First I Laid Siege to My Chloris

AIR XXV   *anon.*

At the tree I shall suf-fer with plea-sure; — Let me go where I

will, — In all kinds of ill, I shall find no such fur-ies as these are. —

Courtiers, Courtiers, Think It No Harm

AIR XXVI

anon.

MACHEATH

Man may es - cape from rope— and gun; Nay, some have out -

- lived the doc - tor's pill; Who takes a wo - man

must be un - done; That bas - i - lisk is sure to— kill. The

fly that sips trea-cle is lost in the sweets, So he that tastes wo - man,

wo - man, wo - man, He that tastes wo - man, ru - in__ meets.

A Lovely Lass to a Friar Came

AIR XXVII

anon.

LUCY

Thus when a good hus-wife sees a rat In her trap in the morn-ing tak - en, With plea - sure her heart goes pit - a - pat, In re- vénge for her loss of bac - on. Then she throws him To the dog or

(1.)

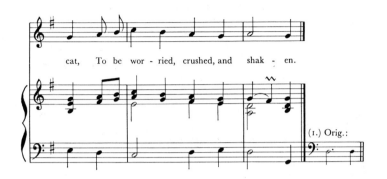

cat,   To be   wor - ried, crushed, and   shak -   en.

(1.) Orig.:

'Twas When the Sea Was Roaring

AIR XXVIII   *G. F. Handel*

LUCY

How cru - el are__ the trai - tors   Who lie__ and swear in

jest,____   To cheat__ un-guard - ed crea - tures   Of

vir - tue, fame, and rest!____   Who-ev - - er steals a

shil-ling,   Through shame the guilt con-ceals;_____ In love_ the

per - jured vil - lain With boasts the theft_ re - veals._____

The Sun Had Loosed His Weary Teams

AIR XXIX   *anon.*

The first time at___ the look-ing glass The moth-er sets her

daugh-ter, The i - mage strikes the smi - ling lass With

self - love ev - er af - ter. Each time she looks, she, fon - der

grown, Thinks ev' - ry charm grows strong - er; But a - las, vain

maid, all eyes but your own Can see you are not young - er.

How Happy Are We

AIR XXX

anon.

When you cen-sure the age, Be cau-tious and sage, Lest the court-iers of-fend-ed should be; If you men-tion vice or bribe, 'Tis so pat to all_ the tribe, Each cries, "That was lev-eled at me."

Of a Noble Race Was Shenken

AIR XXXI

Thomas D'Urfey

LUCY

Is then his— fate de-creed, sir?

(VIOLIN)

Such a man can I think of quit - ting?

When first we met, so

(VIOLIN)

You'll Think, E'er Many Days Ensue

AIR XXXII   *anon.*

LOCKIT

You'll think, e'er man - y— days en - sue, This sen - tence

(1.)

not se - vere; I hang your hus-band, child, 'tis true, But with him

hang your care. Twang   dang   dil - lo   dee

(1.) Orig.:

London Ladies

AIR XXXIII

Thomas D'Urfey

MACHEATH

If you at an of - fice so - lic - it your due, And would not have mat - ters neg-lect - ed, You must quick-en the clerk with the per - quis - ite too, To do what his du - ty di - rect - ed. Or

would you the frowns of a la - dy pre - vent, She too has this pal - pa - ble fail - - ing; The per - quis - ite soft - ens her in - to con - sent; That rea - son with all is pre - vail - - ing.

All in the Downs

AIR XXXIV

Pietro G. Sandoni

POLLY

Thus when the swal - low, seek - ing prey, With -

- in the sash is close - ly pent, His con - sort

with be - moan - ing lay, With - out sits

pin - ing for th'e - vent. Her chat-t'ring lov - ers

all ___ a - round her skim; She heeds them

not (poor ___ bird); her soul's with him.

Have You Heard of a Frolicsome Ditty

AIR XXXV

anon.

MACHEATH

How hap - py could I be with ei - ther, Were
But tol de rol, [tol de rol lol - ly, O

t'oth - er dear charm- er a - way. But while you thus tease me to -
tol de rol, tol de rol lay, But tol de- rol tol de rol

- geth - er, To nei - ther a word will I say,
lol - ly, O tol de rol, tol de rol lay.]

Irish Trot

AIR XXXVI

anon.

I'm bub-bled I'm bub-bled. Oh how I am trou-bled! Bam-

-bouz-led, and bit! My dis-tres-es are dou-bled. When you

come to the tree, should the hang-man re-fuse,— These

fing - ers, with plea - sure, could fast - en the noose.

Cease Your Funning

AIR XXXVII

anon.

POLLY

Cease your fun-ning; Force or cun-ning Nev-er shall my heart tre-pan.

All these sal-lies Are but mal-ice To se-duce my

con - stant man. 'Tis most cer-tain By their flirt-ing

Good Morrow, Gossip Joan

AIR XXXVIII

anon.

LUCY

Why how now, Mad-am Flirt? If____ you thus must chat-ter, And are for fling-ing_ dirt, _____ Let's try who best can

spat - - ter, ma - dam Flirt! Why how now, sau - cy

jade? Sure — the wench is tip - sy! How can you

see me — made — — — — — — — — — — The

scoff of such a gyp - - sy? Sau - cy jade!

Irish Howl

AIR XXXIX.   *anon.*

POLLY

No pow'r on earth can e'er di - vide The knot that sa - cred love hath tied. When par - ents draw a - gainst our mind, The true - love's knot they fast - er__ bind. Oh, oh ray, oh am - bo - rah__

The Lass of Patie's Mill

AIR XL

anon.

I like the fox shall grieve,— Whose mate hath left— her side, Whom hounds, from morn to eve,— Chase o'er— the coun - try wide. Where can my lov - er hide? Where

cheat __ the wa - ry __ pack? If love be not his guide, ___

(1.)

He nev - er __ will __ come back.

(1.) Orig.:

If Love's a Sweet Passion

AIR XLI

Henry Purcell

When young at the bar you first taught me to score, And bid me be free of my lips, and no more, I was kissed by the par-son, the squire and the sot; When the

guest was de - par - ted, the __ kiss __ was __ for - got. But __

(2.)

his kiss was so sweet, and so ___ close-ly he ___ pressed, That I

(1.) Orig.: (2.) Orig.:

lang-uished and pined till __ I grant-ed, the rest.

South Sea Ballad

AIR XLII

anon.

My love is all mad-ness and fol-ly,____ A-lone I lie, Toss tum-ble, and cry, What a hap-py crea-ture is Pol-ly!____ Was e'er such a wretch as I!____ With rage__ I red-den like

scar-let,＿＿ That my dear in-con-stant var-let,＿＿ Stark

blind to my charms, Is lost in the arms Of that jilt, that in-veig-ling

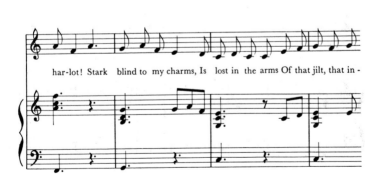

har-lot! Stark blind to my charms, Is lost in the arms Of that jilt, that in-

Packington's Pound

AIR XLIII

Sir John Pakington(?)

- oth - er's de - ceit. But if by mis - hap They fail of a chap, To keep in their hands, they each oth - er en - trap. Like pikes, lank with hun - ger, who miss of their ends, They

bite their com - pan - ions and prey on their friends.

Lillibulero

AIR XLIV

Henry Purcell(?)

The modes of the court so com-mon are grown, That a true friend can hard-ly be met; Friend-ship for in - terest

(1.)

is but a loan, Which they let out for what they can get. 'Tis

true, you find Some friends so kind, Who'll give you good coun - sel them-

- selves to de - fend. In sor - row - ful dit - ty They prom - ise, they

pi - ty, But shift you for mon - ey, from friend to friend.

(1.) Orig.:

Down in the North Country

AIR XLV

anon.

What gud - geons are— we men! Ev' - ry wo - man's eas - y— prey. Though we— have felt— the— hook, a - gain——— We bite, and they be - tray. The bird that hath been trapped, When he

hears his— cal - ling— mate, To her— he— flies, a -

- gain he's clapped ——— With-in the— wir - y—— grate.

A Shepherd Kept Sheep

AIR XLVI

anon.

MRS. TRAPES

In the days of my youth I could bill like a dove,

fa la la fa [la la fa la la lad - dy], In the

(VIOLIN)

days of my youth I could bill like a dove, Like a

spar - row   at   all   times   was   rea - dy   for   love.

[Fa   la   la   la   la   lad - dy,   fa   la   la   la   lad - dy,

(VIOLIN)

fa   la   la   la   fa   la   la   la   lad - dy.]   The

(1.)

One Evening Having Lost My Way

AIR XLVII

anon.

I'm like a skiff on the o - cean tossed, Now high, now low, with each bil - low borne, With her rud - der broke, and her an - chor, lost, De - sert - ed and all for - lorn._____ While thus I lie roll - ing and

toss-ing all night, That Pol-ly lies sport-ing on seas of de-light, Re-

-venge, re-venge, re-venge,— Shall ap-pease my rest-less sprite.—

Now Roger, I'll Tell Thee, Because Thou'rt My Son
AIR XLVIII   *anon.*

Oh Bessy Bell

AIR XLIX

anon.

POLLY

LUCY

What then— in love— can wo - man do? If—

POLLY

we— grow fond they shun us. And when we fly— them,

LUCY

they— pur - sue, But leave us when they've won us.

Would Fate to Me Belinda Give

AIR L

John Wilford

A - mong the men, co - quets we find, Who court by turns all wo - man - kind; And we grant all____ their hearts____ de - sired, When they are flat - tered, when they are

flat - tered, when they are flat - tered and___ ad - mired.

Come, Sweet Lass

AIR LI

anon.

Come, sweet lass, Let's ba - nish sor - row Till to - mor - row;

Come, sweet lass, Let's take a chirp-ing glass.

glass. Wine can clear The va - pors of de -

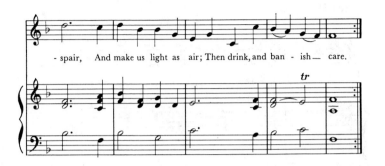

- spair, And make us light as air; Then drink, and ban - ish — care.

The Last Time I Went O'er the Moor

AIR LII

anon.

LUCY: Pol - ly__ sues. 'Tis Lu - cy__ speaks. Is thus true love__ re -
POLLY:

LUCY: - quit - ed? My heart is__ burst -ing.__
POLLY: Mine too__

LUCY: breaks. Must I__
POLLY: Must I__ be__ slight - ed?

(1.)

(1.) Orig.:

Tom Tinker's My True Love

AIR LIII

anon.

MACHEATH

Which way shall I turn me? How can I de-cide? Wives, the

day— of— our— death, are as fond as a bride.

One wife— is too much for most hus-bands to hear, But

two— at— a— time there's no mor - tal can bear.

This way, and— that way, and which way I— will, What would

com - fort the— one, t'o - ther wife would take ill.

I Am a Poor Shepherd Undone

AIR LIV

anon.

POLLY

When my he-ro in court ap-pears, And stands ar-raigned for his life,_____ Then think of poor Pol - ly's tears; For ah! Poor Pol - ly's his wife._____ Like the sai-lor he holds up his

Ianthe the Lovely

AIR LV
John Barrett

When he holds up his hand ar - raigned for his life, Oh think of your daugh - ter, and think I'm his wife! What are can - nons, or bombs, or clash - ing of swords? For

A Cobbler There Was

AIR LVI   anon.

LOCKIT

Our-selves, like the great, to se - cure a re - treat, When

mat - ters re - quire it, must give up our gang; And

good rea-son why, Or, in - stead of the fry, Ev'n

Peach-um and I, Like poor pet - ty ras - cals, might

hang, hang; Like poor pet - ty ras - cals, might hang.

Bonny Dundee

AIR LVII

anon.

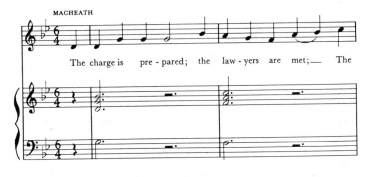

MACHEATH

The charge is pre-pared; the law-yers are met;— The

judg-es all ranged (a ter-ri-ble_ show!) I go, un-dis-mayed, for

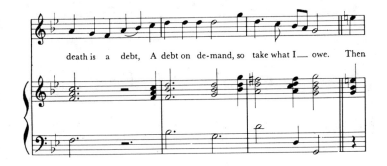

death is a debt, A debt on de-mand, so take what I__ owe. Then

fare-well my love —dear charm-ers, a - dieu.— Con - tent - ed I

die. 'Tis the bet - ter for— you. Here ends all dis - pute— the

rest of our lives,— For this way at once I please all my— wives.

Happy Groves

AIR LVIII

John Barrett

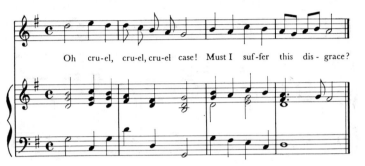

Oh cru-el, cru-el, cru-el case! Must I suf-fer this dis - grace?

Of All the Girls That Are So Smart

AIR LIX

Henry Carey

Of__ all the friends in__ time of grief, When threat'-ning

Death looks grim-mer,__ Not one so sure can bring re-

lief, As__ this best friend, a__ brim-mer.__

Britons Strike Home

AIR LX

Henry Purcell

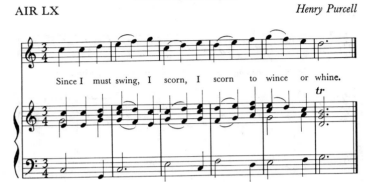

Since I must swing, I scorn, I scorn to wince or whine.

Chevy Chase

AIR LXI

anon.

But now a-gain my spi-rits sink; I'll raise them high with wine.____

To Old Sir Simon the King

AIR LXII

anon.

But val-or the strong-er grows, The strong-er liq-uor we're drink-ing. And

how can we feel our woes, When we've lost the trou-ble of think-ing?

Joy to Great Caesar

AIR LXIII

Michel Farinelli

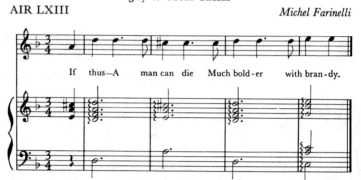

If thus—A man can die Much bold-er with bran-dy.

There Was an Old Woman

AIR LXIV

anon.

So I drink off this bum-per—And now I can stand the test,_____

And my com-rades shall see that I die as brave as the best._____

Did You Ever Hear of a Gallant Sailor

AIR LXV

anon.

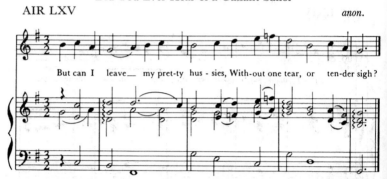

But can I leave— my pret-ty hus - sies, With-out one tear, or ten-der sigh?

Why Are Mine Eyes Still Flowing

AIR LXVI

anon.

Their eyes, their lips, their bus - - - - - ses

Re - call_ my_ love___ Ah, must I___ die?

Greensleeves

AIR LXVII

anon.

Since laws were made for ev'-ry de-gree,— To curb vice in oth-ers as well as me, I won-der we ha'nt bet-ter com - pa-ny Up-on Ty - - - burn tree!___ But

All You That Must Take a Leap

AIR LXVIII   *Lewis Ramondon*

LUCY / POLLY

Would I might be hanged! And I would so

LUCY / POLLY

too! To be hanged with you,＿ My＿ dear,＿ with

MACHEATH

you. Oh leave me to thought! I

fear. I doubt. I trem - ble. I

droop. See,— my— cou - rage is out. No tok - en of

POLLY

MACHEATH

love? See my cou - rage is out. No tok - en of

LUCY

Lumps of Pudding

AIR LXIX   *anon.*

MACHEATH

Thus I stand like the Turk, with his dox - ies a - round; From

all sides their glan - ces his pas - sion con - found; For

black, brown, and fair, his in - con - stan-cy burns, and the

dif - fer - ent beau - ties sub - due him by turns;

(VIOLIN)

put off— your sor - row: The wretch of to - day may be—

hap - py to - mor - row.

Appendix B

Chronology

Approximate dates are indicated by *. Dates for plays are those on which they were first made public, either on stage or in print.

Political and Literary Events	*Life and Major Works of Gay*
1631 Death of Donne. John Dryden born.	
1633 Samuel Pepys born.	
1635 Sir George Etherege born.*	
1640 Aphra Behn born.*	
1641 William Wycherley born.*	
1642 First Civil War began (ended 1646). Theaters closed by Parliament. Thomas Shadwell born.*	
1648 Second Civil War. Nathaniel Lee born.*	
1649 Execution of Charles I.	
1650 Jeremy Collier born.	
1651 Hobbes' *Leviathan* published.	
1652 First Dutch War began (ended 1654). Thomas Otway born.	

1656

D'Avenant's *THE SIEGE OF RHODES* performed at Rutland House.

1657

John Dennis born.

1658

Death of Oliver Cromwell.
D'Avenant's *THE CRUELTY OF THE SPANIARDS IN PERU* performed at the Cockpit.

1660

Restoration of Charles II.
Theatrical patents granted to Thomas Killigrew and Sir William D'Avenant, authorizing them to form, respectively, the King's and the Duke of York's Companies.
Pepys began his diary.

1661

Cowley's *THE CUTTER OF COLEMAN STREET*.
D'Avenant's *THE SIEGE OF RHODES* (expanded to two parts).

1662

Charter granted to the Royal Society.

1663

Dryden's *THE WILD GALLANT*.
Tuke's *THE ADVENTURES OF FIVE HOURS*.

1664

Sir John Vanbrugh born.
Dryden's *THE RIVAL LADIES*.
Dryden and Howard's *THE INDIAN QUEEN*.
Etherege's *THE COMICAL REVENGE*.

1665

Second Dutch War began (ended 1667).
Great Plague.

Dryden's *THE INDIAN EM-PEROR.*
Orrery's *MUSTAPHA.*

1666
Fire of London.
Death of James Shirley.

1667
Jonathan Swift born.
Milton's *Paradise Lost* published.
Sprat's *The History of the Royal Society* published.
Dryden's *SECRET LOVE.*

1668
Death of D'Avenant.
Dryden made Poet Laureate.
Dryden's *An Essay of Dramatic Poesy* published.
Shadwell's *THE SULLEN LOVERS.*

1669
Pepys terminated his diary.
Susannah Centlivre born.

1670
William Congreve born.
Dryden's *THE CONQUEST OF GRANADA*, Part I.

1671
Dorset Garden Theatre (Duke's Company) opened.
Colley Cibber born.
Milton's *Paradise Regained* and *Samson Agonistes* published.
Dryden's *THE CONQUEST OF GRANADA*, Part II.
THE REHEARSAL, by the Duke of Buckingham and others.
Wycherley's *LOVE IN A WOOD.*

1672
Third Dutch War began (ended 1674).
Joseph Addison born.
Richard Steele born.
Dryden's *MARRIAGE À LA MODE.*

1674

New Drury Lane Theatre (King's Company) opened.
Death of Milton.
Nicholas Rowe born.
Thomas Rymer's *Reflections on Aristotle's Treatise of Poesy* (translation of Rapin) published.

1675

Dryden's *AURENG-ZEBE.*
Wycherley's *THE COUNTRY WIFE.* *

1676

Etherege's *THE MAN OF MODE.*
Otway's *DON CARLOS.*
Shadwell's *THE VIRTUOSO.*
Wycherley's *THE PLAIN DEALER.*

1677

Aphra Behn's *THE ROVER.*
Dryden's *ALL FOR LOVE.*
Lee's *THE RIVAL QUEENS.*
Rymer's *Tragedies of the Last Age Considered* published.

1678

Popish Plot.
George Farquhar born.
Bunyan's *Pilgrim's Progress* (Part I) published.

1679

Exclusion Bill introduced.
Death of Thomas Hobbes.
Death of Roger Boyle, Earl of Orrery.
Charles Johnson born.

1680

Death of Samuel Butler.
Death of John Wilmot, Earl of Rochester.
Dryden's *THE SPANISH FRIAR.*
Lee's *LUCIUS JUNIUS BRUTUS.*
Otway's *THE ORPHAN.*

1681

Charles II dissolved Parliament at Oxford.

Dryden's *Absalom and Achitophel* published.

Tate's adaptation of *KING LEAR*.

1682

The King's and the Duke of York's Companies merged into the United Company.

Dryden's *The Medal, MacFlecknoe,* and *Religio Laici* published.

Otway's *VENICE PRESERVED*.

1683

Rye House Plot.

Death of Thomas Killigrew.

Crowne's *CITY POLITIQUES*.

1685

Death of Charles II; accession of James II.

Revocation of the Edict of Nantes.

The Duke of Monmouth's Rebellion

Death of Otway.

Crowne's *SIR COURTLY NICE.*

Dryden's *ALBION AND AL-BANIUS.*

Born June 30 in Barnstaple in Devon. Attended Barnstaple Grammar School.

1687

Death of the Duke of Buckingham.

Dryden's *The Hind and the Panther* published.

Newton's *Principia* published.

1688

The Revolution.

Alexander Pope born.

Shadwell's *THE SQUIRE OF ALSATIA.*

1689

The war of the League of Augsburg began (ended 1697).

Toleration Act.

Death of Aphra Behn.

Shadwell made Poet Laureate.

Dryden's *DON SEBASTIAN*.
Shadwell's *BURY FAIR*.

1690
Battle of the Boyne.
Locke's *Two Treatises of Government*
and *An Essay Concerning Human
Understanding* published.

1691
Death of Etherege.*
Langbaine's *An Account of the
English Dramatic Poets* published.

1692
Death of Lee.
Death of Shadwell.
Tate made Poet Laureate.

1693
George Lillo born.*
Rymer's *A Short View of Tragedy*
published.
Congreve's *THE OLD BACHELOR*.

1694
Death of Queen Mary.   His mother died.
Southerne's *THE FATAL MAR-
RIAGE*.

1695
Group of actors led by Thomas   His father died. Under guardianship
Betterton left Drury Lane and   of an uncle until 1702.
established a new company at
Lincoln's Inn Fields.
Congreve's *LOVE FOR LOVE*.
Southerne's *OROONOKO*.

1696
Cibber's *LOVE'S LAST SHIFT*.
Vanbrugh's *THE RELAPSE*.

1697
Treaty of Ryswick ended the War
of the League of Augsburg.
Charles Macklin born.
Congreve's *THE MOURNING
BRIDE*.
Vanbrugh's *THE PROVOKED
WIFE*.

1698

Collier controversy started with the publication of *A Short View of the Immorality and Profaneness of the English Stage.*

1699

Farquhar's *THE CONSTANT COUPLE.*

1700

Death of Dryden.

Blackmore's *Satire against Wit* published.

Congreve's *THE WAY OF THE WORLD.*

1701

Act of Settlement.

War of the Spanish Succession began (ended 1713).

Death of James II.

Rowe's *TAMERLANE.*

Steele's *THE FUNERAL.*

1702

Death of William III; accession of Anne.

The Daily Courant began publication.

Cibber's *SHE WOULD AND SHE WOULD NOT.*

Became an apprentice to a silk mercer in London.

1703

Death of Samuel Pepys.

Rowe's *THE FAIR PENITENT.*

1704

Capture of Gibraltar; Battle of Blenheim.

Defoe's *The Review* began publication (1704–1713).

Swift's *A Tale of a Tub* and *The Battle of the Books* published.

Cibber's *THE CARELESS HUSBAND.*

1705

Haymarket Theatre opened.

Steele's *THE TENDER HUSBAND.*

1706

Battle of Ramillies.
Farquhar's *THE RECRUITING OFFICER*.

Ended apprenticeship by agreement with master; returned to Barnstaple.

1707

Union of Scotland and England.
Death of Farquhar.
Henry Fielding born.
Farquhar's *THE BEAUX' STRATAGEM*.

Went back to London as secretary of Aaron Hill.

1708

Downes' *Roscius Anglicanus* published.

Met Pope; published first poem, *Wine*, in May.

1709

Samuel Johnson born.
Rowe's edition of Shakespeare published.
The Tatler began publication (1709–1711).
Centlivre's *THE BUSY BODY*.

1711

Shaftesbury's *Characteristics* published.
The Spectator began publication (1711–1712).
Pope's *An Essay on Criticism* published.

The Present State of Wit, an essay, published.

1712

THE MOHOCKS, not acted, printed in April.

1713

Treaty of Utrecht ended the War of the Spanish Succession.
Addison's *CATO*.

Rural Sports published.
THE WIFE OF BATH (Drury Lane, May 15).
The Fan published.
Became member of "Martinus Scriblerus Club," with Pope, Swift, Arbuthnot, and Parnell.

1714

Death of Anne; accession of George I.
Steele became Governor of Drury Lane.

The Shepherd's Week published.

John Rich assumed management of
Lincoln's Inn Fields.
Centlivre's *THE WONDER: A
WOMAN KEEPS A SECRET.*
Rowe's *JANE SHORE.*

1715
Jacobite Rebellion.
Death of Tate.
Rowe made Poet Laureate.
Death of Wycherley.

THE WHAT D'YE CALL IT
(Drury Lane, February 23).

1716
Addison's *THE DRUMMER.*

*Trivia: or, the Art of Walking the
Streets of London* published.

1717
David Garrick born.
Cibber's *THE NON-JUROR.*

With Pope and Arbuthnot, wrote
*THREE HOURS AFTER MAR-
RIAGE* (Drury Lane, January 16).

1718
Death of Rowe.
Centlivre's *A BOLD STROKE FOR
A WIFE.*

1719
Death of Addison.
Defoe's *Robinson Crusoe* published.
Young's *BUSIRIS, KING OF
EGYPT.*

ACIS AND GALATEA, a masque,
with music by Handel (the composer's first score for an English
libretto), performed privately at
the estate of the Duke of Chandos
at Cannons, near Edgware.

1720
South Sea Bubble.
Samuel Foote born.
Steele suspended from the Governor-
ship of Drury Lane (restored 1721).
Little Theatre in the Haymarket
opened.
Steele's *The Theatre* (periodical)
published.
Hughes' *THE SIEGE OF DAM-
ASCUS.*

Poems on Several Occasions (selected
works, including *DIONE* [not
acted]) published.
Invested profits in South Sea stock
and lost heavily when the "bubble"
burst in October.
"Sweet William's Farewell to Black-
Eyed Susan," Gay's most popular
ballad before the ballad operas,
published.

1721
Walpole became first Minister.

Made the friendship of the Duchess
of Queensberry.

1722

Steele's *THE CONSCIOUS LOVERS.*

Assisted Pope in collating editions of Shakespeare.

1723

Death of Susannah Centlivre.
Death of D'Urfey.

Accepted appointment as Commissioner of State Lottery; kept post until 1731.

1724

THE CAPTIVES (Drury Lane, January 15).
"Newgate's Garland," a ballad, published.
Jack Sheppard hanged at Tyburn in November.

1725

Pope's edition of Shakespeare published.

Jonathan Wild hanged at Tyburn in May.

1726

Death of Jeremy Collier.
Death of Vanbrugh.
Law's *Unlawfulness of Stage Entertainments* published.
Swift's *Gulliver's Travels* published.

Swift visited England in the summer, lodged frequently with Gay. Most of Gay's extant letters after this time are to Swift.
"Molly Mog," a ballad, published.

1727

Death of George I; accession of George II.
Death of Sir Isaac Newton.
Arthur Murphy born.

The Fables, First Series, published.
Swift came to England during the summer, visiting Pope and Gay at Twickenham.

1728

Pope's *The Dunciad* (first version) published.
Cibber's *THE PROVOKED HUSBAND* (expansion of Vanbrugh's fragment *A JOURNEY TO LONDON.*)

THE BEGGAR'S OPERA (Lincoln's Inn Fields, January 29).
POLLY suppressed in December (published by subscription in March 1729).

1729

Goodman's Fields Theatre opened.
Death of Congreve.
Death of Steele.
Edmund Burke born.

1730

Cibber made Poet Laureate.
Oliver Goldsmith born.
Thomson's *The Seasons* published.
Fielding's *THE AUTHOR'S FARCE*.
Fielding's *TOM THUMB* (revised as *THE TRAGEDY OF TRAGEDIES*, 1731).

Revision of *THE WIFE OF BATH* (Drury Lane, January 19).

1731

Death of Defoe.
Fielding's *THE GRUB-STREET OPERA*.
Lillo's *THE LONDON MERCHANT*.

ACIS AND GALATEA (Lincoln's Inn Fields, March 26).

1732

Covent Garden Theatre opened.
George Colman the elder born.
Fielding's *THE COVENT GARDEN TRAGEDY*.
Fielding's *THE MODERN HUSBAND*.
Charles Johnson's *CAELIA*.

Died in London, December 4.

1733

Pope's *An Essay on Man* (Epistles I–III) published (Epistle IV, 1734).

ACHILLES (Covent Garden, February 10).

1734

Death of Dennis.
The Prompter began publication (1734–1736).
Theobald's edition of Shakespeare published.
Fielding's *DON QUIXOTE IN ENGLAND*.

THE DISTRESSED WIFE (Covent Garden, March 5).

1736

Fielding led the "Great Mogul's Company of Comedians" at the Little Theatre in the Haymarket (1736–1737).
Fielding's *PASQUIN*.
Lillo's *FATAL CURIOSITY*.

1737
The Stage Licensing Act.
Dodsley's *THE KING AND THE MILLER OF MANSFIELD.*
Fielding's *THE HISTORICAL REGISTER FOR 1736.*